THE PRICE OF OUR VALUES

THE ECONOMIC LIMITS
OF MORAL LIFE

The Price of Our Values

AUGUSTIN LANDIER
DAVID THESMAR

The University of Chicago Press
Chicago and London

The University of Chicago Press, Chicago 60637
The University of Chicago Press, Ltd., London

Published 2025
Printed in the United States of America

34 33 32 31 30 29 28 27 26 25 1 2 3 4 5

ISBN-13: 978-0-226-82708-7 (cloth)
ISBN-13: 978-0-226-82709-4 (e-book)
DOI: https://doi.org/10.7208/chicago/9780226827094.001.0001

Library of Congress Cataloging-in-Publication Data

Names: Landier, Augustin, author. | Thesmar, David, author.
Title: The price of our values : the economic limits of moral life / Augustin Landier, David Thesmar.
Description: Chicago : The University of Chicago Press, 2025. | Includes bibliographical references and index.
Identifiers: LCCN 2024053615 | ISBN 9780226827087 (cloth) | ISBN 9780226827094 (ebook)
Subjects: LCSH: Economics—Moral and ethical aspects. | Utilitarianism—Moral and ethical aspects. | Social values—Economic aspects. | Self-interest. | Decision making—Moral and ethical aspects.
Classification: LCC HB72 .L35 2025 | DDC 174/.4—dc23/eng/20241230
LC record available at https://lccn.loc.gov/2024053615

♾ This paper meets the requirements of ANSI/NISO Z39.48-1992 (Permanence of Paper).

Contents

Preface

One summer, a group of hikers discovers, in the wilderness of Oregon, a cave with astoundingly well-preserved Native American pictograms. They notify National Park Service rangers, and within a few days, archaeologists flock in from all over the world. The cave is found to connect with a vast network of underground dwellings, the vestige of an ancient troglodytic population. In many of these caves, archaeologists find a wealth of well-preserved artifacts that shed light on the religion, family structure, and political customs of this lost civilization. A cemetery is found in the vicinity, with tombs decorated with richly carved stones, along with a monument that indicates the presence of a spiritual site. The legacy of an entire civilization, which disappeared 2,500 years ago, is spread almost intact over a few square miles, nestled in the scenic beauty of the Oregon mountains. It is quickly established that this is North America's most significant archaeological site, on par with Machu-Picchu in Peru. Various revelations about the site excavation, including its astonishing technological advance for the period, make newspaper headlines. In a matter of months, streaming channels put together documentaries. Archaeologists and reporters write international bestsellers about the discovery.

This is not just great news for historians, but also an amazing economic opportunity. Travel guides devote large sections to the site, which is so rich that it takes three full days just to see its main highlights. Tourists from all over the world start coming to the location. But it is remote, and accommodation is lacking. Investors thus take an interest in the area. According to their business plans, if properly developed, the area could attract more visitors, every year, than the Grand Canyon. Forecasted revenues are in the billions of dollars. This would be a boon for the local economy: tens of thousands of local jobs will be created. Among the main beneficiaries will be local Native American tribes, who are struggling economically. Of course, a lot of investment is necessary. Motels, luxury resorts, golf courses, and a small airport need to be set up. The local highway needs to be extended by fifty miles. For the region, this could be just the beginning of a sustained economic boom.

Who should benefit from this find? Some economic commentators compare it to the discovery of natural resources. It is a windfall and therefore should not be given for free to private investors. In a white paper, a Washington, DC–based think tank proposes to auction the license to commercially exploit the site. Provided that constraints on property development are made as minimal as possible, and that the auction is competitive and open to international bidders, the projected revenue is estimated at around $100 billion. To maximize the impact of this windfall on human lives, the proceeds would then fund a large nongovernmental organization (NGO) helping the world's poorest nations.

Of course, these plans raise concerns. Some members of the local Native American tribes oppose the exploitation of the area because it is, after all, the sacred land of their ancestors—an allegation consistent with the consensus of archaeologists. Some historians agree that site access should be very severely restricted. They expect mass tourism to permanently damage both the archaeological site and the surrounding wilderness. For them, economic profits should not be a priority. In an open letter to the *New York Times*, prominent East Coast intellectuals demand that the federal government nationalize the discovery to preserve its purity, concluding: "Our responsibility is to shield this unique historical site from the corrosive forces of greed." They worry that economically struggling locals will sell their land to financial investors, to make a quick profit. Environmentalists have already drafted lawsuits against property developers. Some extreme groups plan to occupy the site and stage violent protests.

***

This story is fictional, cobbled together from a handful of actual stories that really happened. (The discovery of the Lascaux cave in southwestern France in 1940 prompted many of the issues described, for example.) As the example shows, economics is not just spreadsheets and dollar signs. Many economic opportunities involve a balancing act between material desires and moral aspirations. Such tensions arise in all areas of life: Are we ready to give up our vacations abroad in the name of climate change? Should we boycott goods produced in countries that do not respect human rights? Is it immoral to invest our savings in oil companies? To get food delivered by an undocumented immigrant who is not adequately paid? Should governments subsidize museums rather than help other, poorer countries?

Whether we like it or not, our moral values often clash with economic concerns. The resulting tensions make us uncomfortable, not merely because they exist, but also because they are typically unvoiced in polite society. Accordingly, we end up making decisions without a clear understanding of the path we choose—or, perhaps, because we simply want the uncomfortable question to go away. In the face of those tendencies, this book is an intervention, not only to speak the existence of these tensions, but to offer a modestly more elevated way of thinking about them.

Often, our choices are guided by strong principles and emotions—by moral values. Yet, limited resources impose inevitable trade-offs, costs that we must face. It is painful to admit it, but dedicating more to one endeavor always means turning away from another. Our thesis, then, is that *to be fully ethical, our moral decisions must transparently confront their cost implications.* By making these tensions explicit, the book offers a form of couple's therapy: a way of better communicating between our moral aspirations and our inner *Homo economicus* (our materialistic self).

Take our introductory example. The archaeological site is a unique piece of world heritage, to which we owe respect and deference. Local Native American tribes, and more generally all of humankind, have a moral claim on it. Also, why should private, presumably wealthy, investors profit from something (the remains of an ancient civilization) that they have not created? At the same time, it is impossible to ignore the economic part of the equation. Restoring the ruins, learning more about the civilization, maintaining the site for visitors: all of this must be paid for. Once this happens, it becomes hard to prevent hotels and parking lots from being built to host archaeologists and tourists. Jobs will be created, tax dollars will be raised that will serve the local population. As much as it is absurd to ignore the sanctity and the majestic beauty of this discovery, it makes very little sense to completely dismiss the economics.

***

Economists have a toolbox to deal with these moral dilemmas; we wrote this book because we think it is often inadequate. This toolbox goes by the wonky name of "utilitarianism," an ethical system born in England at the end of the eighteenth century. It counts major philosophers as its champions: Jeremy Bentham, John Stuart Mill, Robert Sidgwick, nowadays Peter Singer, and many others. Effective altruism, an influential movement today on US campuses and in Silicon Valley, is its modern incarnation. To make things simple, this philosophy defines the common good as the sum of the pleasures of all humans. A decision is good if it increases mankind's aggregate happiness. It is a universalist moral system: it urges us to take the "point of view of the universe," to equally weigh the happiness of all humans, and possibly animals as well. The think tank proposal, in our introductory example, strictly follows the logic of utilitarianism: it ensures that the discovery maximizes the material well-being of as many people as possible, starting with those who have nothing. Economists embrace utilitarianism because it fits well with the logic of efficiency: the maximum of goodness is obtained by allocating resources to those who need them the most. If one can make as many people as possible better off, one is morally obligated to do it.

These ethics are, however, too simplistic to truly capture the dilemmas that interest us. Intuitive examples of when this moral system fails are not hard to find. For instance, most of us balance our obligations to all human beings (as universalists) against duties to our community, however broadly defined (family, friends, neighborhood, nation). Being fully impartial does not feel "right," because our community holds legitimate moral claims over our actions. Peter Singer describes his own struggle between intuitive ethics and the utilitarian moral compass he has spent his life articulating. When his mother was diagnosed with Alzheimer's disease, he paid for private nursing care for her. What seems to most of us a normal display of filial love goes against utilitarianism since, with the same amount of money, Singer could have saved many lives in the poorest regions of the world.[1] The philosopher is, however, probably the only one who thinks he behaved immorally.

Another difference between people's practical ethics and utilitarianism is the reliance on principles. Economists, when asking themselves if a set of actions is right, focus on the impact of these actions on the common good: they are "consequentialist." But most people would disagree: principles matter. Sticking to good rules, whatever the consequences, is often the right thing to do. Think of Tomas, the main character of Milan Kundera's *The Unbearable Lightness of Being*. Tomas is a successful surgeon working in postwar Czechoslovakia. Outraged by the collaboration of Czech communists with the Soviets, he publishes an article attacking them. Embarrassed by this affair, the hospital manager asks Tomas to write a retraction, which the regime will keep secret unless Tomas creates more problems. Tomas rejects the offer, loses his job, and becomes a window cleaner. Clearly, in this example, Tomas's action has no impact on the world. Whether he writes the retraction or not would not end the totalitarian regime. And no one will ever know if he does. Though it feels to most of us that his attitude is morally right, a utilitarian would disagree since the only effect of his action is to hurt himself, at no benefit to anyone else.

There are many other instances where utilitarianism goes against our moral intuitions. For instance, people value freedom as an end in itself, even when it is self-destructive. Works of art and natural landscapes are not just resources to be exploited but pieces of heritage that we need to conserve and respect. This book will give many such examples.

***

Okay, but if utilitarianism is not the moral compass, what alternative do we offer? Crucially, our approach acknowledges the pluralism of values. Moral dilemmas are the stuff of tragedies; they do not have a single answer. Good people, reasonable people, often disagree when it comes to defining the "common good." Even professional moralists will never agree. According to the philosopher David Chalmers, they are not even trying to: "Philosophical arguments typically lead not to agreement but to sophisticated disagreement."[2]

In this book, we try to construct greater sophistication through deliberation. We will describe different situations in which moral values and economic costs collide (equality, free trade, freedom, responsible capitalism, and so forth). For each one of these, we will provide the perspectives of different moral doctrines. Some may emphasize principles, others duties to our community or our heritage, others different views of fairness, freedom, and so on. Our goal here is not to sell a prepackaged ethical system but to offer a framework for processing moral values while taking economic constraints into account.

To repeat our core argument: Even though there are things that, as political philosopher Michael Sandel puts it, "money can't buy," all moral decisions have a cost: choosing one path always involves forgoing others.[3] It is not immoral, then, but instead healthy and necessary to integrate economic concerns into our moral decisions. However, doing so requires rationally considering several ethical viewpoints. Our inner ethicist tends to get in the way of this; it wants to give some sort of moral monopoly to one set of values (religious, philosophical, political). Instead, our approach calls for a reasoned, careful layout of alternative doctrines. Then, and only then, can we decide which philosophy, which value, best lines up with our aspirations and engage in constructive discussions with those who hold different views.

The flip side of this is, in our view, equally important: economic decisions, personal or collective, are often loaded with moral implications. It would be absurd to ignore them. It matters to each of us when we decide whom to work with, what to consume, and where to invest our savings. When making these choices, we express not only our economic preferences but also our moral values.

Such moral tensions are pervasive in debates about economic policies. In these discussions, economic specialists often apply, consciously or not, the utilitarian moral framework: a net greater good is a reason to do something. Take, for instance, the consensus of economists in favor of free trade. It is based on a simple utilitarian worldview: free trade increases the size of the pie even while it creates losers. So, let's just tax the winners, compensate the losers, and all will go well. Like all economic policies, however, international trade is not just a transfer; it comes with an array of moral consequences: segmenting the population into winners and losers, submitting people to tougher competition, changing the productive status quo that many care about, and so on. These implications cannot be ignored under the pretext that one will "compensate the losers." Not only is it hard to do, but more important, it does not solve many of the moral issues.

This is just an example: most economic policies are designed by advisors who use the utilitarian framework, at odds with the practical ethics of most people. Even though many economists understand this, utilitarianism is the default view to which they spontaneously come back. This limits the relevance of their recommendations, as noted by Nobel laureate Angus Deaton: "When pressed, we [economists who write public policies] usually fall back on an income-based utilitarianism. We often equate well-being with money or consumption, missing much of what matters to people. In current economic thinking, individuals matter much more than relationships between people in families or in communities."[4] Accordingly, it is not surprising that people disagree so often with economists.[5] In our view, the moral misalignment between the ethics of economic experts and the moral preferences of everyone else is a key problem in our democracies.

***

So, let's get started. Before we discuss the various dilemmas, we will start with a brief, cherry-picked, history of economic thought. There is, in our collective history, a propensity to separate our materialistic self from our moral self. We need to reconcile these two selves: we are both moral and economic beings at the same time. This will help us acknowledge and accept the tensions between our material desires and our moral instincts. Doing so, however, is not as simple as it looks. Different situations elicit different types of tensions. This is what the rest of this book will be about.

1
Making Morals and Economics Meet

The Oliveira Da Silva family live in Brazil. Their story has been related in a *New York Times* article.[1] The article depicts the family's mother within the walls of a modest home, cradling her younger son, Levi. The fate of Levi depends on access to a groundbreaking but exorbitantly priced therapy for spinal muscular atrophy. Levi's older brother, Lorenzo, suffers from the same genetic condition but did not receive treatment. Nearly paralyzed and mute, he is a silent testament to the merciless progression of the disease that would await Levi if untreated. For Levi, the possibility of a normal life comes with a staggering cost—$1.7 million for a single treatment of the drug Zolgensma. This price tag is enormous given the financial capabilities of Brazil's public health system, which balked at the sum, sparking a legal battle that resulted in a poignant victory for the Da Silva family.

Of course, in cases like this one, our heart screams for action, for compassion, for the value of a child's life is infinite, and the cost to save it inconsequential. The thought of withholding a treatment that could prevent Levi's paralysis is unthinkable. We instinctively rally behind the cause of saving a child.

At the same time, we know that our spontaneous support for Levi is only the emotional side of a complex ethical debate. A Brazilian congresswoman's words summarize the hidden tragedy of the situation: "We also cannot be irresponsible and approve something that is not sustainable in the long term." The act of giving to one can mean taking from others. As we delve deeper, our reason tells us that ignoring economic constraints is simply dishonest—resources *are* finite. Brazil's public health system is strained under the weight of demands. The reporter calculates that court-ordered expenditures on Zolgensma could have funded more than four million doses of a life-saving vaccine. Where does one draw the line?

In fact, Levi's case demands that we confront the hard question: Where do we draw the limits of our ideals when faced with the harsh constraints of economics? A "whatever it takes" approach to such moral dilemmas is not a viable solution. We cannot simply follow our emotional impulses to decide what is right or wrong. Acknowledging the cost side of the equation is necessary. Moral, even.

The cognitive psychologist Daniel Kahneman distinguishes between two modes of thinking: System 1 (the gut feeling, which is fast but often incorrect) and System 2 (the rational calculus, more effective but slower).[2] The method of this book consists of highlighting and acknowledging moral/economic trade-offs when they arise, and doing so calmly and rationally. Put System 1 on pause, and take our time to engage System 2. Given the complexity of these trade-offs, however, we will need to make room for a variety of ethical perspectives and moral values. In a nutshell, if we do not want System 1 to take over our moral thinking, System 2 requires constructive and rational deliberation between moral viewpoints. In plain English, dealing with moral/economic trade-offs requires us to be value-pluralist.

We start this chapter by explaining why bridging values and economic constraints can be difficult. When tragedies such as Levi's situation arise, our instinctive response is to categorize individual decisions into somewhat hermetic categories: on one hand, decisions where moral imperatives should prevail (this is our emotions speaking—our System 1); on the other hand, situations where the pursuit of our economic interest guides us. The rest of the chapter explains how to bring the two spheres together, to reason both economically and morally at the same time.

The Dichotomy between Markets and Morals

When we face a moral/economic tension, our instinctive moralist, our emotion-based System 1, tends to switch to "whatever it takes" mode. This is because we intuitively put morals and economics into separate categories of our lives. Indeed, we are taught (through education) to distinguish between situations in which the logic of the market should prevail and those from which, on the contrary, it is to be banished. When we offer our seat to a pregnant woman in the subway, we do not ask to be paid (even if she seems to belong to a well-to-do social category). Only a sociopath would do that. But when we sell a house, it is natural to sell it to the highest bidder. That another, less wealthy prospective buyer is more deserving or needs the house more is irrelevant. The rule of the game, for a house seller, is to extract the largest possible price. In some situations, it is the social norm to be 100 percent profit-driven, and no one will criticize us for it. In others, this seems unacceptable.

Psychologist Paul Tetlock has an explanation for why we are instinctively repelled by the idea of balancing morals and economics.[3] According to him, there are three types of trade-offs. *Routine* trade-offs are between two economic decisions (Should I buy tomatoes or yogurt? Should we invest in a railway or an airport?). The market is the place where the resolution of these trade-offs usually takes place, peacefully intermediated by prices. Trade-offs between moral values are *tragic* (Should Antigone bury her brother or obey her king?). There is no peaceful resolution, but they are openly debated across millennia of literature; they are the stuff of life. Finally, trade-offs between moral and economic objectives are *taboo*. Why are they taboo? Tetlock proposes several explanations. First, economic discussions, or any type of rational calculus, when it comes to values activate a defense of the sacred. Morality is historically the domain of religion: putting dollar signs on moral values is an insult to God, a blasphemy. Another explanation given by Tetlock is signaling to others: the mere evocation of money when ethics are at stake sends the message that one's moral compass is broken. To go back to Levi's case, mentioning the cost of the treatment is perceived as insensitive: only a person who lacks basic empathy would run an economic analysis to decide whether or not to save a child's life.

Another explanation is that money degrades morality itself; it diminishes its worth. It diverts us from the good life. For example, putting a price tag on a friendship makes it a market transaction and therefore a less valuable relationship. Modern philosophers in the "virtue ethics" tradition (put simply, philosophers who think that the purpose of life is to forge one's character, one's virtues) make a similar argument. In *What Money Can't Buy*, Michael Sandel discusses many real-life situations in which the introduction of a market destroys the intrinsic worth of goods.[4] For example, he describes a company in China that apologizes on behalf of its customers, a firm that specializes in ghost-writing wedding speeches, and more. The mere fact that the apology and the wedding speech are purchased makes them worthless. Sandel's view is that money forces people to think in utilitarian terms, a distraction from the purpose of a life worth living: the development of one's virtues. For Sandel, morals and economics are incompatible because they belong to deeply incompatible moral systems.

Adam Smith's Thought Experiment

Economists have been a foundational part of the notion that markets and morality should exist separately. The eighteenth-century economist Adam Smith invites us to a provocative thought experiment: a market where only the logic of self-interest rules, where there is no pretense: buyers and sellers do not engage in exchange out of empathy, and everyone knows this. Adam Smith contends that this hypothetical market will produce the greatest good to the greatest number. "It is not from the benevolence of the butcher, the brewer, or the baker that we expect our dinner, but from their regard to their own interest. We address ourselves, not to their humanity but to their self-love, and never talk to them of our own necessities but of their advantages."[5] The objective of this thought experiment was not to describe the world as it is but to show that self-interest is enough to make the market work.

The message of Smith has also been understood as: "You should not feel guilty to be amoral in a market context, because this makes things actually work better." This was a new idea. For many thinkers before Smith, the pursuit of individual interest was perceived as a source of chaos and violence (think of Thomas Hobbes's view of the state of nature as a "war of everyone against everyone").[6] Smith's *The Wealth of Nations* offers a complete reversal of perspective. In the market, one selfishly works to the best of one's ability to make a profit. And because making profits implies satisfying customers, this quest for profit allows everyone to benefit from the work of others. Somewhat paradoxically, the right attitude here is to be amoral, to maximize one's own interest.

Sociologist Albert Hirschman proposed a related, but slightly different, argument than Smith: the market brings peace because it satisfies people's appetite for turbulent passions.[7] Economic interactions encourage a specific vice (the lure of profit) and even give it a kind of monopoly. Making money is a calm and harmless passion when compared with religious fanaticism or the appetite for power. In some sense, the market acts as a focal point for our bad instincts; it cleans us morally.[8]

Of course, Smith never claimed that all human actions are governed by self-interest. He did not believe—far from it—that there was no room in our lives for love, courage, honesty, and other virtues. He even wrote a famous work, *The Theory of Moral Sentiments*, before *Wealth of Nations*. But with the latter work, he isolates a sphere where the logic of self-interest can prevail: the market. Smith understood that traditional virtues were also part of the ethos of capitalism.[9] However, his separate treatment of the wealth of nations and moral sentiments paved the way for a dichotomy that would eventually prevail in the mainstream of economics. Milton Friedman's famous saying that the only "social responsibility of business is to increase its profits" falls right into that tradition (we will discuss this in more detail in chapter 8).

When Morals and Economics Collide

While the separation of economics and morals can sometimes be a useful simplification, it is not helpful in most of the day-to-day decisions that we must make. In practice, some employees want to find meaning, not just money, in doing their jobs. They accept lower pay for occupations that bring dignity and fulfillment. Consumers look not only at prices but also at the conditions (ethical or not) under which goods are produced. Some investors refuse to invest in companies that they feel harm society or the environment. Others look for "impact," to make a difference in the world. Voters may oppose reforms that increase GDP (as in the debate on protectionism) but which they feel unfairly hurt parts of the population or jeopardize national identity.

It's not just individuals. Institutions of modern capitalism routinely mix values and economics, at odds with the view that one can separate them. Companies these days want to be "socially responsible," and some even contend that profit should not be their only goal. While it is reasonable to doubt the sincerity of these claims, large swaths of the postindustrial economy, such as education, health care, or culture, are operated by nonprofits (universities, hospitals, museums, even banks) that have a mission (to educate, save lives, preserve artworks, finance the community) but cannot ignore economic constraints or the forces of competition.

Levi's predicament is another stark example of a collision between moral values and economics. While our gut instinct is to spend whatever it takes to save him, this instinct ignores a necessary trade-off: the medicine he needs is so expensive that saving Levi would come at the cost of many "statistical" lives (lives that would be saved by vaccines that cannot be purchased). After deliberating, we may decide that saving Levi is the right thing to do (for instance, because, on balance, we decide that putting a price tag on human life can lead to dangerous moral drift). But it would be bizarre, if not outright immoral, not to at least consider the consequences of this decision for other Brazilian citizens.

The Roots of Utilitarianism

The example of Levi suggests a natural way to deal with these moral/economic trade-offs: to balance moral gains (funding Zolgensma, saving x number of lives) and moral costs (causing y number of deaths as a result of not funding vaccines). Then, make the decision that has the largest net benefit (fund Zolgensma if $x > y$). This rather cold calculus goes by the name of utilitarianism and was first laid out by Jeremy Bentham at the end of the eighteenth century. Bentham thought that people seek only one thing: to maximize their *utility*: "Nature has placed humanity under the governance of two sovereign masters, pain and pleasure. It is for them alone to indicate what we should do, as well as to determine what we will do. . . . A thing is said to promote the interest, or to be for the interest of an individual when it tends to add to the total sum of his pleasures: or, what amounts to the same thing, to diminish the total sum of his pains."[10]

In other words, the utility of an action is determined by its ability to produce pleasure and reduce pain. This is reminiscent of hedonism, the philosophy of ancient Greece that would urge its disciples to "seize the day," except with a new twist: the optimizing part. Bentham's premise is that human beings choose their actions by *calculating* the pleasure or pain these actions will bring them. Bentham's humans are well equipped to inhabit the market sphere envisioned by Smith since they only think about maximizing their personal pleasures—they are not altruistic, they are driven by self-interest.

Of course, and this is what interests us here, Bentham thought that there was more to the "good life" than focusing on maximizing one's own pleasures. Using his psychological model of people, he created a criterion for what constitutes the "common good," the kind of outcome that a benevolent government should seek. According to his view, an action is good if it increases the sum of all individual utilities. For Bentham, the common-sense principle of "the greatest happiness for the greatest number" is the ethical choice, the moral compass of a good government. To this day, this calculus is routinely used by economists to assess the legitimacy of new or existing policies. They call it "welfare analysis."

This approach to the common good also provides a possible definition of individual virtue. According to utilitarianism, a person who seeks to promote the common good abstracts from self-interest and internalizes all the positive and negative effects their actions may have on *all* other human beings (whether they live next door or on the other side of the world; whether they are family members or complete strangers). Today, Bentham's philosophy is not only alive among economists interested in cost-benefit analysis but also influential as a doctrine of the good life—as we will discuss in the next chapter.

Let us reiterate the difference between descriptive and normative utilitarianism. Bentham did not see this selfless attitude as a realistic model of human behavior. He thought that pure individualistic hedonism was much closer to reality. But at the same time, he strongly felt that the role of economists and political leaders was to help design rules that maximize the sum of all utilities. Thus, his philosophy, and his personal commitments, were driven more by idealism than by pleasure. He called for the abolition of slavery and corporal punishment. He was an early advocate of animal rights. In this sense, Bentham the philosopher was much less cynical than Bentham the psychologist.

The Limits of Utilitarian Calculus

Utilitarianism thus offers a natural way of integrating our economics and morals into our decisions. The good decision, the one we should aim for, would be the one that increases the sum of pleasures. But deep down, we all feel that our moral decisions cannot be reduced to such a simple criterion. In many economic/moral dilemmas, we do not just weigh costs and benefits, we use other moral compasses as well. Exploring these alternative ethics, and how they emerge in many economic situations, is the purpose of this book. This is what we will do in the following chapters. To give the reader a preview, we provide a brief list here of limitations of the utilitarian calculus that will be recurrent themes:

- *Principles matter*. To deal with dilemmas, we often rely on principles, rather than thinking about the precise consequences of our actions on people's welfare. These principles are grounded in what we consider to be right (from religion, culture, reason, or personal introspection), irrespective of real-world consequences. Some things are simply not negotiable. Russian novelist Dostoyevsky's *Crime and Punishment* is a forceful expression of this thesis. The main character, Raskolnikov, a penniless student in nineteenth-century St. Petersburg, kills his landlady. The plot twist is that he justifies his crime with "reasonable" arguments. The woman is an ugly pawnbroker, someone of lower moral quality. Killing her makes the world a better place. The utility gains of her debtors would far outweigh the loss of her life. Once his murder is accomplished, however, Raskolnikov is overcome by remorse. He confesses his crime and accepts his punishment. This is Dostoyevsky's proof that utilitarianism leads to moral nihilism. We will discuss the moral foundations of deontology (ethics based on principles) in more detail in chapter 2, as well as in chapters 8 and 9.
- *Pleasure is not the only guide to our moral actions.* If we really think about it, we cannot just care about pleasure. Philosopher Jon Elster illustrates this through a thought experiment. If we were offered a pill that eliminated our ability to experience guilt, would we take it? In Bentham's world, the answer should be a clear yes, because we would thus eliminate displeasure and increase the scope of our pleasurable actions. Raskolnikov would have avoided collapsing

psychologically and going to jail. But most of us would likely refuse to take the pill, for the simple reason that pleasure and pain are not the only foundations of moral choices.[11] Similarly, assume that a company designs a new machine that takes the form of a black box. Provided you sit in it, the machine would give you the maximum amount of pleasure, permanently—but nothing else. Very few of us would think of purchasing this machine.[12] Why is this? Economist Tyler Cowen argues that we care about a multiplicity of values, such as beauty, freedom, personal accomplishment, and so on. A life devoted to pleasure only is incomplete. This leads Cowen to advocate against the consumption of alcohol and drugs (even safe ones), because they only give pleasure.[13]

- *The set of moral values is diverse*. Bentham's virtuous man cares about the well-being of all human beings. This is a praiseworthy goal, but it is not the only one that matters to people. For many, liberty, beauty, tradition, or a vibrant and fraternal community are at least as important as the well-being of humans. Leveraging decades of research in psychology and anthropology, Jonathan Haidt identifies in his work six cardinal moral values: compassion, liberty, loyalty to the in-group, fairness, authority, and sanctity.[14] We all care about all of these moral values to some extent, but the relative weights we place on each of them vary quite a bit. Utilitarians score high on the values of compassion and fairness—as do self-reported progressives. Libertarians mostly care about freedom (liberty) as an end in itself, even if it leads some of us to hurt ourselves through addiction or errors of judgment. Some people respect the sacred value of their cultural heritage and are willing to sacrifice their well-being to preserve it (loyalty, sanctity). We all agree that fairness matters but often disagree about what is fair, as in the debate between equality of opportunities versus equality of conditions. The wide range of our moral values will be discussed in chapters 3–7.
- *The accounting of pleasures and pains is hard to do*. This last line of criticism challenges utilitarianism not on philosophical but on practical grounds. Let us give an example of the pitfalls of utilitarian calculus.

In a recent book, the utilitarian philosopher William MacAskill wants to show that voting is moral, in the sense that it improves the sum of utilities.[15] He starts with an estimation that each voter has a 1 in 60 million chance of being the one person affecting the outcome of a federal election. He then argues that if your preferred party gets into power, you can expect an aggregate gain for the United States of at least $140 billion. His argument is the following: assume that your party, compared to the opposite party, can increase the efficiency (in terms of the objectives you care about) of government spending by 1 percent, over four years. Then, this corresponds to about $140 billion in total. Then, the expected welfare gain of voting would be $140 billion, but only in one case out of 60 million (since this is your likelihood of affecting the outcome of the election). If you are a true utilitarian, you will compare the cost of voting (wasting a couple of hours) to your expected impact on society ($140 billion divided by 60 million, or $2,000). Clearly, that's enough for a utilitarian to go and vote. MacAskill's argument is logically sound and somewhat provocative (it is "optimal" to vote, you do not need to do it out of duty). But it also highlights the difficulties of evaluating the consequences of one's actions: How much should we trust the 1-in-60-million probability estimate? Do people really evaluate the gain to society of their preferred candidate at $140 billion? We develop this issue—that evaluating the consequences of one's actions is hard—in more detail in chapter 6, in our discussion of globalization.

A Plea for Value Pluralism

Naturally, we did not invent this list. It may not even be exhaustive. Since the dawn of history, religious individuals, philosophers, and laypeople have developed ethical systems that significantly diverge from the Benthamian system promoted in economics. In a 2014 survey of professional philosophers,[16] only 25 percent considered themselves "consequentialists" (aligned with the idea that the moral good consists of maximizing total well-being). Another 26 percent claimed to be "deontologists" (believing that morality should be grounded in just principles). Eighteen percent labeled themselves "virtue ethicists" (Michael Sandel's group). The rest had a more nuanced view: 8 percent thought more than one approach should be considered, 5 percent were undecided, and so on. Overall, the landscape of professional philosophers is quite diverse. Throughout the book, we will summon the different schools of thought to help us think about the various moral/economic dilemmas we will encounter.

We will also lean on the wisdom of regular people. We are all, in our everyday lives, intuitive moralists. In our practical ethics, we have developed preferences, sometimes well articulated, sometimes vague, that will determine how we react to trade-offs between moral and economic goals. In every chapter of this book, we will look at survey participants to see how they think about the various dilemmas through a variety of questions. Their answers inform our discussions.

Eliciting People's Moral Preferences

We argue that our surveys will help us probe the *moral preferences* of people, how they trade off moral values and economic implications in various settings. Crucially, this implies two important assumptions that we need to discuss here. First, as argued by economists Gary Becker and George Stigler in a famous paper, we assume that people's moral preferences are somewhat *stable*, reflecting the fact that people tend to have consistent tastes across contexts.[17] For instance, if Emily is more compassionate than average, she is more likely to donate to charities, but also more likely to scrap her weekend plans to help a friend. If Bob cares more about order than average, a large fraction of the money he donates will be for law and order–related charities. At work, Bob is also more likely to expect that his subordinates do exactly as instructed. Overall, to be of any use, the concept of moral preference will require that individuals have a consistent way of solving trade-offs between morals and economics. Becker and Stigler made this point in the classic utilitarian framework (utility of material consumption). We argue that the same should apply when we discuss moral/economic dilemmas.

Second, moral preferences are different from *beliefs*. Emily may be compassionate but may not believe that bed nets are effective against malaria. She thus donates less to charities that specialize in this type of intervention. Bob mostly cares about order and authority. Therefore, when casting his vote, his belief in the candidates' abilities to implement law and order policies will be crucial. This belief may be informed by the candidates' public speeches, party affiliations, Bob's own prejudices, and so forth. They may be right, or wrong, but they should not be confused with Bob's preferences, his taste for an orderly society, and his respect for authority. In this book, we focus on preferences, rather than beliefs.

To separate these two, our survey questions will rely on "thought experiments": hypothetical situations where we do our best to control their beliefs about how the world works. These hypotheticals are self-contained but simple situations that can be grasped easily. An advantage of this approach is to minimize the influence of participants' knowledge and beliefs and to distill their actual preferences. This "experimental" approach is inspired by the classic trolley problems discussed in ethics classes since the 1970s. The purpose of these stylized moral dilemmas was initially to foster classroom discussion about ethics (we will discuss trolley problems in more detail in chapter 2).

For the purpose of this book, we ran two separate surveys. The first one is a pool of US, French, and German participants (2,000 in each country), surveyed by the polling firm Kantar in June 2021. The second consists of 939 US participants, polled in December 2022 through the online platform Prolific.

Shedding Light on Moral Preferences: A Preview

Before concluding this chapter, let us give an example of hypothetical situations that we subject our survey participants to. At the beginning of the COVID crisis, in the spring of 2020, along with Parinitha Sastry and David Sraer, we recruited 200 US residents online and asked them the following question:[18]

> You are an emergency physician. Two patients, Sam and Tom, are brought in at about the same time. They are both suffering from advanced lung infection as a result of COVID-19, and need to be transferred to the ICU. Both men are young. Sam has no comorbidities, so you estimate that care will increase his probability of survival from 60 to 80%. Tom has had a history of recurrent pneumonia since childhood, so emergency care will increase his probability of survival from 40 to 80%. Because of the outbreak, the hospital is overcrowded: there is only one bed available. What do you choose?
>
> 1. Send Tom to the ICU,
> 2. Send Sam to the ICU,
> 3. Send the first person who came to the emergency room to the ICU.

This question presents a clear, self-contained, hypothetical (the triage of a patient), where the consequences of each decision are clearly defined and not left to the participant's imagination. A utilitarian would focus on efficiency and choose to treat Tom. Since Sam is more likely to make it on his own, this choice maximizes the expected number of survivors. Someone who values fairness above efficiency would opt for answer 3: treat patients in the order in which they arrived.

The key message from the data is that participants' moral values are diverse. Forty-nine percent of the respondents followed the logic of efficiency, while fairness considerations prevailed for another 37 percent of them. It is likely that by varying survival probabilities, we would obtain different answers. For example, if Tom's probability of survival, without treatment, was zero (instead of 40 percent), we would expect respondents to choose option 1 more often. If it happened (we did not test this), it would mean that some participants trade off fairness concerns (they give up on the order of arrival criterion) for more efficiency.

Throughout the book, in many different situations, we will find that survey participants do think in terms of such trade-offs.

Wrapping Up, Going Forward

Morals and economics show considerable overlap. Sure, not everything has a price. But all decisions, even moral decisions, have a cost that needs to be taken into consideration. When we donate to charities, we must choose whom to help, which causes we care the most about, and therefore which battles we will not fight. Governments face the same trade-offs all the time, and they become especially salient when budgets are debated and voted on. Spending more on defense or education is good, but it hurts spending on criminal justice or health care. In the private and public spheres, such moral trade-offs are omnipresent. But how do we deal with them?

While economists have a tool (utilitarianism) to deal with such dilemmas, it cannot be the sole moral compass. To be sure, it can be useful in some situations, but centuries of religion, philosophy, and practical ethics have come up with alternative principles. Moral/economic dilemmas are complex, and their answers are mostly elusive. It is preferable to debate the different viewpoints and give different approaches a voice than to apply the same prepackaged criterion to all situations. One size does not fit all.

While we summon the knowledge accumulated by professional thinkers from various fields of social sciences, we also probe the practical ethics of laypeople through two large surveys conducted in the United States, Germany, and France. These surveys confirm that participants express a plurality of values, as in the example we gave above. In line with the approach of this book, the answers people give to our questions acknowledge the trade-offs and reflect the plurality of points of view.

We begin by exploring the first kinds of moral/economic dilemmas that most people think of, those involving a conflict between our self-interest and the well-being of others.

2
Altruism

In recent years, effective altruism (EA) has become a hugely influential movement. It promotes the idea of maximizing through a rational approach the amount of good that can be achieved by an individual. The movement is deeply inspired by the utilitarian approach of economics, which combines consequentialism (what matters is outcomes) and universalism (the good of saving a life does not depend on whether it is the life of a relative or that of an unknown person). Despite these "-isms," EA is not confined to the ivory tower: it has become a mass movement, influential among charities, popular among billionaire philanthropists, and, more important, drawing large crowds of young disciples at convention centers around the United States. It is not an academic sideshow but rather, for many, a way of life, almost a religion.

Effective Altruism: Impartiality and Efficiency

The first key argument of EA is that altruism should be completely impartial. A pioneer is the Australian philosopher Peter Singer, who developed the argument in a famous 1972 essay. There, Singer invites us to a famous thought experiment. Assume you are walking by a shallow pond and see a child drowning. Even if that means getting your clothes wet or being late to an appointment (but not dying yourself), no one would hesitate to dive into the pond and rescue the child. This is because the value of a life saved is so high. Then, Singer argues, the same logic should apply to saving lives in poor societies:

> It makes no moral difference whether the person I can help is a neighbor's child ten yards away from me or a Bengali whose name I shall never know, ten thousand miles away. . . . The fact that a person is physically near to us, so that we have personal contact with him, may make it more likely that we shall assist him, but this does not show that we *ought* to help him rather than another who happens to be further away. If we accept any principle of impartiality, universalizability, equality, or whatever, we cannot discriminate against someone merely because he is far away from us (or we are far away from him).[1]

In other words, if we ground it in reason, altruism ought to be universalist. There used to be a time when it was impossible, for the compassionate, to help people who were too far away. There was limited awareness, and few reliable institutions had a global reach. It was more effective to focus on the community. But this excuse is no longer valid, Singer argues. One of the good things about globalization is that our donations can be effectively directed to help the poor at the other side of the world. As a result, people fortunate enough to live in rich nations have a moral duty to transfer some of their incomes to poor societies, even in faraway places.

The second pillar of EA is the focus on *efficiency*. As in traditional utilitarianism, maximizing the aggregate good is at the core of this conception of ethics. Doing some good does not quite "cut it": the truly ethical person needs to optimize. The philosopher William MacAskill, a pillar of the EA community, explains in his manifesto *Doing Good Better* how to pick the best ways to make a difference. MacAskill invites people to review how they can make their impact on others as positive as possible. The book's framework is explicitly based on the economic idea of optimizing efficiency.[2] A provocative application of this concept is what effective altruists call "earning to give." If you have a skill that is highly valuable in the labor market, you should earn as much income as you can and give it away to efficient charities, rather than spend your time trying to directly help others.

For all its logical soundness, this approach goes against the moral intuitions of most people. We illustrate this tension by asking our US survey participants to think about the following hypothetical:

> Nick is asking advice to solve a moral dilemma. He is just graduating from college, and would like to help people in poor countries.
>
> As his first job, Nick wants to enroll as a construction worker in an NGO that builds hospitals in Africa. However, a philosopher friend tells him that he could do more good by (1) taking a high paying job in Wall Street, and (2) giving a large portion of his earnings to this NGO. The NGO could then use the money to hire several workers instead of one.
>
> What advice would you give to Nick?
>
> 1. Follow his heart and enroll with the NGO to directly be involved in charity work.
> 2. Follow his friend's advice, because it is indeed more impactful.

Only 29 percent of the survey participants chose the second answer. Thus, only a minority of participants found "earn to give," one of the main recommendations of effective altruism, convincing. Note that this skepticism was not driven by less compassionate participants. Indeed, we asked our survey participants, in a separate question, whether they feel that "compassion for those who are suffering is the most crucial moral value," on a scale from 1 to 5.[3] We find that respondents who care more are neither more nor less likely to recommend "earning to give." People do not equate generosity with the precepts of EA.

That is not surprising. In charitable work, our moral intuition tells us that writing a check is not enough. Directly experiencing human contact with the people we want to help seems morally superior. Also, the fact that the logic of optimization delivers a unique rational priority list seems somewhat odd in the context of charity. Many readers of this book would balk at the idea that some suffering, even if happening to people close to us, simply does not deserve our attention, because we can more efficiently spend our time on other people. They would challenge the idea that maximizing the number of lives saved per dollar spent is a valid compass for our charitable efforts.

Also, the idea that sacrificing some people is okay if it saves others goes against the idea that people have fundamental rights that are nonnegotiable. Very few people would find it acceptable if a surgeon harvested organs from a healthy patient who came in for a check-up in order to save several victims of a car accident who needed urgent organ transplants. Another piece of evidence for such aversion to "instrumental harm" is that people distrust politicians who are willing to sacrifice some citizens to promote the welfare of others.[4]

Last, many of us believe that we hold special obligations toward those closest to us: our family, friends, and community. When these people are in need, it feels entirely natural and certainly not "irrational" to be more willing to share our wealth and time with them compared to strangers.

In this chapter, we argue that the type of altruism promoted by standard economic analysis is akin to EA. It emphasizes universalism and effectiveness. Although rooted in an old tradition and sound arguments, this view of altruism is not the only one. As we just saw, it is not shared by the general population, nor is it the only acceptable one from an ethical viewpoint. Taking into account the actual values of people requires economics to limit its normative ambition (saying what "good altruism" is) and leaves room for the moral preferences of the population.

Let us avoid misunderstandings. We do not mean to say here that academic economics ignores the "altruism of real people." That would be incorrect. There is a very large literature that seeks to analyze the way people care about each other in various settings. Some have run experiments, others have analyzed data, and have found numerous situations in which economic agents are generous and cooperative (by donating to charities, cooperating in the workplace, and so on). We briefly review some of these findings in this chapter, but this is not our main point here. What we contend is that *applied* economic analysis has a very specific view of what altruism should be, a view very similar to EA: striving for universal equality, while maximizing efficiency. As a result, economists tend to ignore or dismiss alternative value systems as irrational, or even "less moral."

Utilitarian Ethics

At the very beginning of EA is, of course, the work of Jeremy Bentham. To make things simple, let us say that utilitarian ethics are grounded in two principles. The first is that individuals maximize their self-interest. As we discussed in chapter 1, this is not just a description of how people behave but a "life advice," an injunction to enjoy existence as much as one can. It is an ideology of liberation, of self-expression. People are encouraged to free themselves from the constraints of tradition and social norms and do what they think is good for them—in Benthamian ethics, maximize their utilities. But, of course, Bentham does not stop here. He is a public intellectual interested in promoting social welfare. So, he adds a second principle: that the government designs institutions so as to maximize the sum of people's utilities. What makes Bentham a true universalist is that this sum is *unweighted*. Everyone, merchant or aristocrat, master or slave, teacher or child, counts the same in the eye of the benevolent ruler. This second principle also makes Bentham a *consequentialist*: a government policy is good insofar as it actually improves the sum of people's utilities. Good intentions, without results on people's utilities, do not count.

Thus, while individuals have the right to do what they please, the government is in charge of promoting equality. This is the line of thinking that led Bentham, and then his pupil John Stuart Mill, to fight against aristocratic privileges and for the emancipation of women, slaves in faraway colonies, and children.

Like effective altruism, modern economics is built on Bentham's legacy: individual rights to maximize self-interest and a universalist superego. While these ethics are perfectly sensible on many counts, they do not represent the only way to think about morality. For one thing, they are not representative of the general population's ethics, and for another, they are not the only philosophically coherent moral system out there.

In what follows, we will discuss the three pillars of EA (self-interest maximization as a legitimate purpose for the individual, universalism, and consequentialism), how they fit with human nature, and possible alternatives that have been discussed in the history of ideas.

Not Personal, Just Business

Why is it that economics assumes and even promotes the pursuit of individualistic self-interest as a legitimate purpose? We have already mentioned the legacy of the Enlightenment and the emancipation of the individual in the eighteenth-century liberal tradition. But another important reason is Adam Smith's idea that self-interest is consubstantial with the very idea of markets. It is not just that markets work well with selfish agents, but also that they do *not* function well if people are not greedy.

Adam Smith formalized in *The Wealth of Nations* the idea that altruism is not just superfluous but actually toxic to market efficiency. The reason is that the market works best when people are impartial. The *ethos of business* is not to choose suppliers we feel sorry for or whose society we enjoy, but to choose the ones who have the best and cheapest product. If we need to choose between two potential recruits who are paid the same wage, the selfish logic of markets is to choose the most productive one. We will be able to gain market shares from our competitors and increase our profits. Hiring the less productive candidate because he is the most in need of money or because we like him may lead us to smaller profits despite a superior product.

Empathy and favoritism thus stand in the way of economic efficiency. In chapter 1, we were reminded of Smith's famous citation: "We address ourselves, not to [the baker's or the butcher's] humanity but to their self-love." But then he adds: "and *never talk to them of our own necessities but of their advantages*." Empathy and altruism should be toned down. Moral indifference is a normative prescription in economics: this is the way one should behave for a market to function properly.

This insight has had profound implications. For the following two centuries, we economists have largely worked under the assumption that individuals are mostly self-interested, sometimes blurring the line between the normative and the descriptive status of this assumption: Is it telling us how people are or how they ought to be? Most of our models, most of our policy recommendations, were based on the idea that people would respond to external circumstances by selfishly maximizing their utility of consumption. British economist F. Y. Edgeworth famously argued in his 1887 treatise that "the first principle of economics is that every agent is actuated only by self-interest."[5] Somewhat annoyed by this principle, Amartya Sen—a Nobel Prize–winning economist as well as a philosopher—notes that "this view of man has been a persistent one in economic models, and the nature of economic theory seems to have been much influenced by this basic premise."[6]

To this day, most of our models, especially the ones we use to analyze policy, assume that agents act in their own self-interest. Even when cooperative behavior arises, it is often because people care about their personal well-being. For example, if you make a taxi reservation through a digital platform, not canceling your reservation will damage your *rating*. An economist would immediately think of this sort of reputational concern, which can lead you to behave prosocially only because that is in your own self-interest. Another version of this selfish altruism is "virtue signaling." In some models, agents behave nicely to gain other people's trust. Sometimes, the logic is pushed one notch further: individuals act cooperatively to signal their virtue to *themselves*, to boost their self-esteem. Such trivialization of selfishness is a form of moral pessimism that has earned economics its reputation as a "dismal science."

The Criticism of Economics and the Invention of Altruism

The term "altruism" was coined in opposition to this rather bleak view of human nature. Its invention is credited to Auguste Comte, a French intellectual active in the first half of the nineteenth century. Comte came of age during a period of social turmoil. He wrote after the end of absolute monarchy, the French Revolution, and the Napoleonic Wars. He witnessed the rise of industry, which he saw as a force of progress. The ambition of his sociology was to help design a modern society based on scientific principles (he was trained as an engineer) and a new religion. Comte believed it dangerous to promote, as economists and liberals do, the maximization of self-interest as a respectable way of life. He advocated, instead, "altruism," the opposite of egoism. Comte's paradigm was the family: he wished to generalize nonmarket exchanges, in contrast to the "modern anarchy" constituted by the economists' market.

This indictment of the market would later be echoed by another Frenchman, sociologist Émile Durkheim. Along with his German contemporary Max Weber, Durkheim is considered one of the founders of modern social sciences. Like Weber, but using a different lens, Durkheim viewed modernity as a tragedy. With the rise of industry, labor was becoming more and more specialized, and relationships more transactional. In the old social order, individuals were integrated in a web of human relationships: the corporation, the church, and the neighborhood.[7] People were less free, but they had a role to play, duties to fulfill, and multiple daily human interactions. The advent of modernity, according to Durkheim, led to "anomie" (normlessness), a situation in which individuals lost their connections with one another and their purpose. Uprooted from their communities, people became miserable and lonely. The most vulnerable were led to take their own lives (Durkheim's best-known work is a statistical analysis of suicide). For those who survive, the demise of the ancient norms fostered the worst kind of individualism, where individuals were pitted against one another by the forces of competition.

Durkheim shares with Comte a complete rejection of the individualism of economists and the detestation of their discipline. "[Economists] neglected everything that did not relate to the strictly individual life, so that from abstraction to abstraction they were left with only the dismal portrait of the egoist."[8] Clearly, self-interest is the root of the deep acrimony between economics and sociology, dating back to the beginning of these social sciences.[9]

The New Economics of Altruism

Of course, economists do not literally believe that people are only motivated by self-interest. Edgeworth knew his assumption was a crude approximation of reality and seemed to regret it: "The concrete 19th-century man is, for the most part, an impure egoist, a mixed utilitarian."[10] Smith, and even Bentham, emphasized the compassion one feels toward an unfortunate neighbor, or how much we share the pain of our loved ones. "When we see a stroke aimed and just ready to fall upon the leg or arm of another person, we naturally shrink and draw back our own leg or our own arm; and when it does fall, we feel it in some measure, and we are hurt by it as well as the sufferer," Adam Smith remarked.[11]

Since the early 1980s, a large academic literature has taken off that documents altruism in the data. Some of these data come from lab experiments in which people play games with financial payoffs. A famous and stark example is the "dictator game," in which subjects are given an amount that they can freely share with another participant. The participant is just on the receiving end and cannot retaliate if disgruntled (as would be the case in another famous experiment, the "ultimatum game"). In these experiments, participants do exhibit quite a bit of altruism. They are willing to share their gains (typically, about 25 percent) with other participants, even if they expect nothing in return, and even if they do not personally know the person they are giving to.[12]

Yet, Economics Still Sticks to the "Self-Interest" Model

Despite these advances, most of economics still assumes that economic agents are selfish maximizers. This is especially striking in policy-related research. An example is cost-benefit analysis, the goal of which is to evaluate the merits of a policy delivering a public good (such as a highway, a park, or a museum). Such analysis is focused on materialistic well-being. How many hours of leisure will be saved by a highway? How many visitors will a park or a museum have? Such analysis ignores the compassion of people for one another. For instance, people who do not have kids may enjoy seeing children playing in the park. Or members of the community who live far from the highway may empathize with noise disturbances that affect those living nearby. Cost-benefit analysis completely ignores these dimensions.

Another example is the research on "optimal taxation," which typically assumes a government trying to minimize inequality or aiming to raise a given amount of funds. This research assumes that economic agents focus on their material well-being: they dislike taxes because taxes reduce consumption, and they prefer leisure to work. While this model has generated many deep insights, it is a rough approximation of attitudes to taxes. For instance, some people don't mind paying taxes if it helps those in need or if it funds the conservation of nature. Work is not just the flip side of leisure and a source of cash but is a value, a source of fulfillment, a way to contribute to society.

The absence of altruism is particularly striking in the literature on voting behavior. Voting is typically a case where people express their values as well as their self-interest. Yet, to analyze voting behavior, economic models assume that agents only vote in a self-interested way. This leads to lengthy discussions about the "paradox of voting": for a rational, self-interested voter, the costs of voting (the time it takes, the transportation cost, and so on) usually outweigh the expected benefits because the likelihood that one's vote turns out to be "pivotal" (that it changes the outcome of the vote) is extremely small. So, the fact that people vote is described as a puzzle from the perspective of mainstream economic models. The self-interested view on voting also leads to the core result that rich people vote for lower taxes and poor people for higher taxes. But this is very crude, to say the least. Many poor people vote against taxes, and many relatively wealthy voters support higher taxation, likely because they feel they can afford to pay more taxes and reduce the burden on poorer citizens. In line with this view, Amory Gethin, Clara Martinez-Toledano, and Thomas Piketty have shown that since 2010, more people among the top 10 percent of earners in the United States vote Democrat than Republican.[13] A few recent papers have started to incorporate notions of altruism in voting, but this literature is still surprisingly underdeveloped.[14]

Universalism: The Credo of Economists

The second principle (after self-interest) of the ethics of economics is universalism. While individuals are urged to flourish through the maximization of self-interest, a moral superego (represented by the government) should seek to maximize the *unweighted* sum of all utilities. To the moralist, everyone should matter equally.

Why do economists (as moralists) favor universalism? One reason, as we have seen, is instrumental: impartiality is good for economic efficiency. A form of altruism that favors people close to us (geographically, culturally, or genetically) inevitably leads to cronyism and favoritism. It damages economic efficiency, as shown by a large body of research on corporate governance, political connections, family businesses, and so forth.[15] But the main reason why economics favors universalism is moral and historical. It is part of the DNA of the discipline, starting with Jeremy Bentham and John Stuart Mill. Today, it is the implicit moral value that economists promote, for example, by focusing on income equality. Typically, economists are in favor of redistribution schemes through taxes, which do not favor people on other criteria than their need for help. They prefer to rely on such an *impartial* system rather than on individual charity, which they know to be biased toward our social or familial circle.

This repugnance among economists toward "proximity-biased altruism" is rarely explicit. Part of economics is about normative statements (how things ought to be), and universalism is part of the norms economics tries to promote. Montesquieu, here perfectly representative of this economist spirit, explicitly states that he finds it immoral to favor those who are more familiar to us over those who are distant: "If I knew something useful to me, and harmful to my family, I would reject it from my mind. If I knew something useful to my family, and not my country, I would try to forget it. If I knew something useful to my country, and harmful to Europe, or useful to Europe and harmful to Mankind, I would look upon it as a crime."[16]

An economist would say that Montesquieu's chilling impartiality is good for productivity and ethics at the same time: the temptation to favor those close to our hearts must be fought as a conflict of interest. There is a deep connection between the ideal market and a form of meritocratic egalitarianism, which places all individuals on an equal footing, without regard for our private and emotional ties.

The Actual Altruism of People Is Not Universalist

As students of human nature (as psychologists, not moralists), however, economists have long known that human altruism falls short of their universalist ideal. We do indeed tend to favor those who are closer to us, in particular our family, rather than those who are most in need of our help. Our altruism is in practice full of partiality. Smith himself noticed—but did not condone—that human altruism seems much stronger toward people close to us: "After himself, the members of his own family, those who usually live in the same house with him, his parents, his children, his brothers and sisters, are naturally the objects of his warmest affections. . . . The children of cousins, being still less connected [than 'the children of brothers and sisters'], are of still less importance to one another; and the affection gradually diminishes as the relation grows more and more remote."[17]

This insight has been confirmed by modern research on altruism. For instance, in experiments, participants tend to be more generous to people they already know or have had interactions with. More recently, the economist Ben Enke and his coauthors have developed innovative survey techniques to measure universalism in people's practical ethics.[18] For example, they ask survey participants how they would split a hypothetical $1,000 donation between two individuals, one close to them and one more remote. Some of the questions measure global universalism by allowing participants to share the donation between a compatriot and a foreigner. Others measure more "local universalism" (family versus nonfamily members, neighbors versus nonneighbors, and so on). Their survey thus measures the *direction* of altruism, rather than the *quantity* of altruism, since participants are asked to assume that $1,000 will be donated. One might worry that this measure is purely hypothetical, but Enke and his coauthors show that participants give very similar responses when told that their preferred allocation has a nonzero chance of being implemented (that is, when the experimenters actually make the donation). Overall, the simplicity of this survey design makes it easy to implement on large and international samples.

This research documents a strong proximity bias in altruism. On average, about two-thirds of the $1,000 is donated locally, and one-third remotely. Of course, respondents vary a lot in their degree of universalism. Among participants, universalists are more likely to donate money to global NGOs, to be educated, and to invest their retirement money globally. Universalists are not more generous: "localists" (who are on average more religious) give more to *local* actions undertaken by their parish or temple. Universalists are in general less socially integrated: they have fewer friends and fewer relationships and are more likely to be socially isolated and lonely. By embracing humanity as a whole, universalists seem condemned to abandon their loved ones, to rid themselves of their social relations.

Should People Be More Universalist?

Are people wrong to not strictly embrace Benthamian universalism? While the universalist tradition is a legacy of religion and the Enlightenment, centuries of philosophy and sociology also praise investment in the local community and the respect for its traditions. Let us mention a few examples. A whole group of "communitarian" thinkers, often inspired by the Scottish philosopher Alasdair MacIntyre, propose a renewal of Aristotelian ethics, which values traditions and local belonging (to a community, a tribe, a corporation). From this point of view, the individual, insofar as they want to participate in collective life, must de facto embrace the heritage of particular traditions. To be moral is to be rooted in an identity. This identity plays a determining role in the meaning of one's life, one's moral reference points, and one's duties and solidarities.

Political philosopher Michael Sandel, who is in this tradition, formulates this view in the following way: "I can only make sense of my life story by taking note of the stories I am part of."[19] The community is the repository of the integrity and evolution of a tradition. As members of various corporations (for instance, journalists, doctors, mathematicians, or plumbers), our duty is to acknowledge the importance of tradition and the authority of our peers. A life worth living involves accepting the rules and, when necessary, doing one's best to convince our peers to change them. This is because, as individuals, we have not only rights but also duties to protect and care for others. This duty is not only to the entire human race: our community, our nation, and our family also lay legitimate claims on us.

The philosopher Kwame Anthony Appiah also argues about our duty to our community. In *Ethics of Identity*, he explores the tensions between universalist aspirations and belonging to traditions. To him, the struggle is real and personal. Born in London to a Ghanaian father and an English mother, Appiah was educated in Kumasi and at Oxford and now lives in New York. In his book, he dismisses what he calls "extreme cosmopolitanism," the "telescopic philanthropy" of Dickens's character Mrs. Jellyby, who cares more about overseas projects than the chaos of her own household. He insists on the ethical importance of loyalty to the groups with which we are affiliated, whether they are determined by our origins (country, religion, ethnicity, family) or by our existential path (corporation, neighborhood, hobbies).[20]

There is also a long-standing tradition in sociology of praising the virtues of the community. As we said earlier, some of it goes back to the late nineteenth century and the sociology of Émile Durkheim. Durkheim lamented the weakening of community in industrial society, the replacement of "mechanical solidarity" (the ancient order, with its many obligations and relative stagnation) by "organic solidarity" (the modern order, based on individualism, specialization, and transactional relations). With the advent of organic solidarity, the community disappears, and individuals, urged to become "utilitarians" (a contemptuous term for Durkheim), drift into despair and solitude.

The modern embodiment of this insight is the work of Robert Putnam on "social capital." His thesis is that shared identity is a bulwark against the individualism that undermines Western societies. Putnam links this modern loneliness to greater cultural diversity and population movements: too much diversity (which undermines the identity dynamic) in a neighborhood leads, according to him, to a decline in the trust that exists between its inhabitants.[21] The loneliness epidemic in our societies has harmful consequences on health, especially since it is aggravated by the disappearance of certain sectors of economic activity, which leaves the individual isolated economically and morally.

This theme also runs through Anne Case and Angus Deaton's economic bestseller *Deaths of Despair*, which examines the excess mortality of the American working class undermined by deindustrialization: "For many, the institutions that provided support—marriage, church, and community—no longer do; identity and status have been challenged and the meaning of life has been lost. As Émile Durkheim would have predicted, suicides have increased."[22]

Not Everyone Is a Consequentialist

The third and final principle of the "ethics of economists" is consequentialism. In utilitarian ethics, good intentions, sound principles, are not enough. The good of a decision only comes from its real consequences. While this criterion is obvious to most economists, it is quite different from the practical ethics of most individuals. In the general population, good intentions and moral principles matter, irrespective of consequences.

Modern economics does not completely ignore this, but this awareness is confined to altruism research. In the late 1980s, the economist James Andreoni introduced the distinction between "pure" and "impure" altruism.[23] "Pure" altruism corresponds to an individual who values the welfare of others per se. Such individuals are consequentialist: they only care about actions that improve the well-being of others.

"Impure" altruists are people who care about charitable actions for their own sake. Andreoni says that "impure altruists" receive a "warm glow" when they perform a charitable gesture, such as a donation. Whether this donation really changes anyone's life is not the main reason for their action: they are not consequentialist. A dark side of the warm glow might be that the person is just concerned to signal her virtue to others (to gain their trust) or to herself (to enjoy a boost of self-esteem). This interpretation is favored by economists, always inclined to see people as self-interested. But there is also a bright side to the warm glow: it may be the case that the person acts out of a sense of duty.

This distinction between pure and impure altruism turns out to be crucial for charities seeking donations. If a cause is already adequately funded by the donations of others, impure altruists will continue to give, because what matters to them is the act of donating itself. Pure altruists, in contrast, should be less inclined to give. Thus, a charity seeking to raise funds may want to advertise its past accomplishments (if donors are impure altruists) or rather insist on the need for money (if they are pure altruists) to avoid suggesting that the bulk of issues targeted by the charity have been resolved. In order to identify to what extent people are "pure" or "impure" altruists, economists have set up experiments in laboratories or in partnership with NGOs to understand the intensity of this crowding-out effect. They find significant evidence of impure altruism. Actual people are driven not only by results but also by an impulse to do the right thing.[24]

This distinction between pure and impure altruism echoes old philosophical debates. Traditionally, philosophy distinguishes between consequentialist and deontological ethics. Deontological ethics root what is right in principles. One such famous principle is Immanuel Kant's "categorical imperative," whereby an action is moral if this is an action one wishes everyone would adopt. In his words: "I ought never to act except in such a way that I could also will that my maxim should become a universal law."[25] One ought not to lie because a society where everyone lies would be unbearable. One should pick up one's trash on the beach because a society where littering is acceptable leads to polluted seashores. Adherence to this categorical imperative goes against self-interest: whether I pick up my own trash has no material effect on the amount of garbage that lies on the beach when I arrive on it. One small lie might sometimes have clear benefits in terms of its consequences, for instance, when hiding a friend from a person trying to kill them. In that sense, the no-lie imperative is not consequentialist. What matters is whether everyone does follow the rule, but in plenty of cases, breaking the rule might have positive consequences. As a deontological individual, I should, however, be committed to following the rule in all circumstances.

How do people reason? The moral psychologist Jean-François Bonnefon and his coauthors have gathered international evidence based on variants of the "trolley problem." This famous thought experiment, designed by moral philosophers in the 1970s, forces individuals to choose between a status quo where five people will die and an alternative that saves these persons but involves killing one other person. One typically expects consequentialists to prefer the outcome that only leads to one death, while deontological thinkers would opt for the status quo decision, since killing, even to save other people, violates the principle of not using people as means to an end (another of Kant's imperatives).

Depending on the variant of the trolley problem (some involve just flipping a switch to save five people, others involve actively killing an innocent bystander), Bonnefon and his coauthors find that, in most countries, between 20 percent and 40 percent of the people are nonconsequentialists—they refuse to be accomplices to killing.[26] Interestingly, East Asia (especially China) has a much larger fraction of deontological thinkers. The economist Roland Bénabou and his coauthors have looked at a broader range of hypothetical situations.[27] They find a similar percentage of nonconsequentialists but, surprisingly, no consistency within each individual across experimental conditions: the same person can sometimes be a consequentialist, sometimes a deontologist, depending on the context. This finding is in the spirit of this book: there is no single legitimate moral approach to all problems; rather, people's practical ethics vary according to circumstances.

Much more research is needed to understand better when and why people lean on principles to guide their moral behavior and when they think in terms of effectiveness. But two additional facts emerge from the work of Bénabou and his coauthors. First, many of us rely on rules: a large majority of their experimental subjects reject consequentialism at least sometimes. Second, there is *no* correlation between empathy and consequentialist thinking: deontological thinkers are found in equal proportions among generous and relatively selfish people. This echoes our survey question at the beginning of this chapter: those who think that Nick should maximize his impact by working on Wall Street are not "better people."

Hard-Core Consequentialism and Erosion of Moral Values

A heavy dose of consequentialism can lead to dangerous side-effects, including the erosion of moral values in those who adhere to it—this is the "virtue ethics" attack on consequentialism. Many people believe that a fulfilling life, a life with purpose and meaning, requires cultivating one's virtues. Like the bodybuilder who needs to exercise every day and be on a strict diet, the virtuous individual needs to constantly practice in order to stay in "moral shape," to flourish. A danger with the consequentialist calculus is that it sometimes leads to the conclusion that a vice (say, making money on Wall Street) could have good consequences (say, helping build a hospital in Africa faster). Doing good "better" then stands in the way of individual flourishing, blocking the road to character: as idle muscle turns into fat, virtues turn into vices.

Consequentialism not only diverts us from ourselves; it also diverts us from others. By overly fixating on computing consequences and utilities, individuals are steered away from other human dimensions of altruism (emotional, spiritual). The lives of others may become mere statistical concepts instead of being seen as real lives of actual people. This emphasis on abstraction can potentially affect our moral compass over time, pushing us toward a technocratic rather than a compassionate approach to others. This is the message of "care ethics," an approach of ethics (developed notably by feminist authors such as Carol Gilligan and Nel Noddings) that highlights the crucial importance of personal direct relationships.[28] This approach is neither consequentialist (relationships matter, not only abstract moral principles) nor universalist (we have special duties to care for persons close to us, and it is physically impossible to care for everyone). It favors caring and relationships over logic and reason, which are the pillars of effective altruism.

Last, consequentialism is a threat to our autonomy, our free will. Philosopher Bernard Williams explains how reasoning in terms of consequences robs individuals of their abilities to define their plans of life in a coherent way (their "project"). His thought experiment features "Jim" and "George."[29] Jim visits a village in the jungle. In this village, an evil person, Pedro, threatens to kill twenty villagers unless Jim agrees to shoot one villager dead himself. George is an engineer who is offered a well-paid job at an arms manufacturer. His family needs the money, and George knows very well that if he refuses the job, another, less scrupulous engineer will replace him. Both proposals make moral sense from a consequentialist viewpoint, but they collide with the life projects of Jim (say, a nonviolent explorer) and George (say, a pacifist). They infringe on the men's individual autonomy. Put differently, utilitarianism, according to Williams, requires too much impartiality from humans because it forces individuals to give up on the consistency of their characters. It violates their integrity.

An example of consequentialism going off the rails is effective altruism's prescription of "earning to give," already discussed at the start of this chapter. Bright students are encouraged by the EA community to take well-paying jobs in order to donate and maximize their impact. This recommendation, which seems out of line for 71 percent of our respondents, attracts students from top universities, like, for instance, Sam Bankman-Fried, the founder of the now-defunct crypto exchange FTX:

> When Bankman-Fried was in college, he had a meal that changed the course of his life. His lunch companion was Will MacAskill, the Scottish moral philosopher who's the closest thing EA has to a leader. Bankman-Fried told MacAskill that he was interested in devoting his career to animal welfare. But MacAskill convinced him he could make a greater impact by pursuing a high-earning career and then donating huge gobs of money: "earning to give," as EA calls it.[30]

Bankman-Fried became one of the major donors of the effective altruist movement and was tightly connected to its key advocates. When it turned out that FTX was fraudulently using clients' money for speculative investments, EA became the target of intense criticism. The *New York Times* commentator David Brooks highlighted what he thought was the biggest danger of EA, the corrosion of character by money: "If you go to Wall Street mostly to make money for charity, you may turn yourself into a machine for the redistribution of wealth. . . . Taking a job just to make money . . . is probably going to be corrosive, even if you use the money for charity rather than sports cars."[31]

Of course, effective altruists have various fixes to their doctrine that supposedly prevent this kind of reckless behavior. For instance, Will MacAskill rejects pure consequentialism and admits that some deontological elements (for instance, the principle that stealing is forbidden, even for a good cause) should be integrated into our definition of moral behavior.

Altruism: The Great Divide

To summarize, applied economics, by using the utilitarian framework, implicitly promotes a highly specific moral view that combines individual maximization of materialistic self-interest, universalism, and consequentialism. This makes the economic view of altruism quite different from most people's practical ethics. As we have discussed throughout this chapter, people are not only self-interested; they care about their close ones and their communities, and they are not consequentialist. They think in terms of duties (to their community, to their country) as well as rights. They think the practice of doing good matters more than impact.

Economists are more and more aware (through empirical studies) that their moral framework does not provide a good description of people's moral preferences. But they keep using it when performing welfare analysis (usually based on a utilitarian cost-benefit analysis) to decide whether or not a policy is desirable for the population. This back-door normativism (which imposes a specific view on what is the common good) is dangerous, as it creates a gap between a technocratic view of what are the "smart policies" and the aspirations of the population. Out of respect for people's ethics and human nature, economists should learn to integrate the diversity of value systems that exist in the general population. This more pluralistic approach is the one that this book is advocating for.

3
Freedom

In January 2008, firefighters stormed into the home of pop star Britney Spears. She was quickly strapped to a gurney and taken to the psychiatric emergency department. Before this, and for a long time, Spears had been behaving erratically, grappling with bad influences, depression, and alcohol. A few days after her forced hospitalization, a California judge ordered her placement under conservatorship, a legal status designed for incapacitated adults. In the following years, her father became her legal guardian and, as such, the manager of her fortune and her career. He controlled her dating habits and filtered her access to telecommunications. To fight the ruling, she tried to hire a lawyer, only to learn that as an irresponsible person, she had no right to one without a court order. All her requests were denied. As of July 2021, she had lived thirteen years—more than half of her adult life—under the control of a team of guardians and lawyers whom she paid, out of her own pocket, about $1.1 million a year (about twice her personal allowance).[1]

In the summer of 2021, the court finally appointed a lawyer to represent her. In a poignant speech, Spears laid bare the harrowing conditions of her existence under the conservatorship: the concerts she was obligated to perform, the mandatory use of a contraceptive device, and the psychiatric treatments she had to undergo. It is impossible not to be shocked by the tragedy of her years in confinement.

Obviously, there are many examples of deprivation of liberty that are much more dramatic than that of Britney Spears. From the horrors of slavery to the torture of political prisoners, from individuals wrongly incarcerated to those who fall prey to the abuse of cult leaders, there is no shortage of examples of freedom being taken away. But it is precisely because Spears enjoyed comfortable living conditions that her story highlights the value of liberty. With important life decisions taken care of and material needs met, one could expect Spears to be satisfied with her life. She had an enviable job and thousands of devoted fans and was even protected from her own self-destructive impulses. Some may argue that her guardianship was "optimal," maximizing her utility in a Benthamian sense. However, Britney's court statement clearly tells a different story. Being stripped of one's freedom is an earth-shattering event, an ultimate violence, a loss of dignity. Liberty is not just a means to an end (living comfortably), it is an end in itself.

In this chapter, we describe how economic thought has curiously ignored freedom as an end in itself. Unlike philosophy, economics has historically held a mostly *instrumental* view of freedom. It sees freedom as valuable insofar as it is an effective way to reach utilitarian efficiency. Whenever efficiency is at stake, economics tends to lean toward limiting individual freedom or even manipulating people to shield them from their own mistakes. In this chapter, we explore recent debates where the intrinsic value of freedom is disregarded, such as modern paternalism and the discussions surrounding online "echo chambers" and "fake news." But before delving into those examples, let us revisit the roots of freedom as a concept.

The Paradox of Negative Liberty

Freedom is at heart a philosophical concept. It emerges in seventeenth-century European thought with the ideal of individual autonomy: autonomy from the sovereign, from religion, from the community. A first view of liberty defines it as the absence of constraints on individual actions: it is what British philosopher Isaiah Berlin refers to as "negative liberty."[2] Two English thinkers, John Locke and Thomas Hobbes, shared the view that unrestricted negative liberty would lead to its own downfall. They imagined individuals living in a (fictitious) "state of nature" with no constraints. These individuals would end up anything but truly free from external constraints—preyed upon by armed bands and in a perpetual state of stress. In the state of nature, safety or property rights are not guaranteed for anyone.

Hence, Locke and Hobbes concluded that, for the very sake of individual freedom, some limits on freedom must be agreed upon: we cannot live a free life unless constraints limit what others can do to us. French philosopher Jean-Jacques Rousseau famously encapsulated this idea with the formula: "Liberty consists less in doing one's will than in not being subject to that of another."[3] Hobbes, Locke, and Rousseau converged on a similar solution in the form of a *social contract* providing a foundation to the state: all individuals agree on reasonable limits to their freedom. In exchange for restricting what they can do, citizens receive a guarantee of a protected personal space,[4] a bubble of autonomy where they are free to define their identity and act by their own personal rules. This individual autonomy is valued in its own right, and it is the job of the government to ensure its protection. This idea of a social contract, enforced by the government, is a foundational concept in political philosophy, emphasizing the need for a balance between individual liberty and the common good.

Positive Freedom, Negative Freedom

A second facet of freedom is referred to by Isaiah Berlin as "positive liberty." The thinkers promoting this idea highlight that a life of freedom requires acquiring various individual capacities. One is not born free; one becomes a free human being through social interactions and institutions, starting with language. To better understand the distinction between negative and positive liberty, consider the example of freedom of speech: when a person does not face censorship, there is "negative liberty of speech." But to have "positive liberty of speech," this person needs to have developed cognitive abilities and learned how to speak and express ideas. Otherwise, their freedom of speech is more formal than real.

So, the key idea of positive freedom is that, by themselves, individuals are not able to achieve their potential. They need access to education, to opportunities. This requires the removal of social or economic barriers. The philosophers who advocate for positive freedom seek progress toward an ideal version of humankind, striving to lift humans out of their current imperfect state. The struggle for positive freedom consists of changing society, improving the human condition, and freeing humankind from its material constraints, its ignorance, its moral imperfections.

According to Berlin, this reorganization of society on a rational basis is the Enlightenment's essential undertaking. However, this can prove challenging, as individuals' "empirical selves" may resist the march of progress. Thus, it may be necessary to constrain individuals to move forward on this path: some liberties may need to be sacrificed, and if resistance is met, coercion should force people to comply and evolve. As Berlin puts it:

> If I am a legislator or a ruler, I must assume that if the law I impose is rational (and I can only consult my own reason) it will automatically be approved by all the members of my society so far as they are rational beings. For if they disapprove, they must, pro tanto, be irrational; then they will need to be repressed by reason: whether their own or mine cannot matter, for the pronouncements of reason must be the same in all minds. I issue my orders, and if you resist, take it upon myself to repress the irrational element in you which opposes reason.[5]

There are indeed authoritarian accents in the promotion of positive freedom. Before Berlin, the risk of a totalitarian drift in such a project was a source of preoccupation for earlier liberal thinkers. For example, John Stuart Mill was frightened about his French correspondent Auguste Comte when the latter wrote that he saw no good reason to tolerate diversity of opinions in morals and politics more than in mathematics and physics. Berlin shared Mill's sentiment. A Russian Jew who fled the Bolshevik revolution, he saw in the cult of "positive liberty" the germ of the totalitarianism of the twentieth century that so dramatically affected his family. For any system based on reason does not tolerate multiple solutions. It only has one right answer, and reason commands to impose it. Berlin called this attitude "monism," in opposition to pluralism.

Berlin is remembered as the champion of pluralism, valuing the diversity of opinions and advocating for flexible and pragmatic thinking (represented in another one of his famous essays by the fox, in contrast with the monomaniac thought process of the hedgehog).[6] Berlin's work, along with that of other scholars, has brought to light the existence of two distinct liberal traditions: one that prioritizes assisting individuals in achieving the ideals of Enlightenment (the monist society), and another that sees individual liberty as the bedrock of individual rights and promotes a pluralist society. In fact, a truly pluralist liberal society is willing to go as far as accommodating groups that reject individual autonomy. It protects the existence of those who oppose freedom in the name of preserving diversity.[7] This is particularly true regarding freedom of speech, where monism can easily justify restrictions: "I disapprove of what you say, but I will defend to the death your right to say it" runs a famous quote attributed to Voltaire.

Economists and Freedom

Strangely enough for a discipline often accused of worshipping free markets, the treatment of freedom in modern economics is limited. In economic theory, freedom mostly has an *instrumental* value. This is because economics is so heavily influenced by its founding father, Jeremy Bentham, for whom freedom has no intrinsic value: it does not increase one's utility. It may be a *means* to achieve more happiness, as when Jack is allowed to choose his vacation or his career so as to match his tastes better. But it does not intrinsically *bring* happiness:

if someone else, who knows Jack well enough, was making the same choices for him, Jack would be equally happy. There can even be "too much freedom," in the sense that private decisions get in the way of economic well-being. In this case, mainstream economics insists that liberties should be restricted by regulation, manipulated by the tax system, or shackled by invisible nudges designed to steer individuals on the right path.

To be fair, over the course of the twentieth century, economists have done their share in the fight for freedom, particularly in the controversies after World War I that opposed them to advocates of economic planning and totalitarianism more generally. The Austrian school was on the front line of the battle for liberty. Joseph Schumpeter in *Capitalism, Socialism, and Democracy* defends freedom as an instrument of innovation and economic progress. In the famous chapter on destructive creation, freedom to innovate allows the bold entrepreneur to replace incumbent producers. But creative destruction is disruptive to society. Schumpeter's worry is that, in the long run, people's appetite for stability will slow the pace of innovation and growth.[8] By giving up freedom, people would give up on the promises of technology and material improvements. For Friedrich von Hayek and Ludwig von Mises, economic freedom allows the best possible satisfaction of individual needs. A central planner cannot know in detail the needs of each consumer, of each firm. It would require an almost infinite capacity to store and manage information. In contrast, a decentralized economy, composed of free agents and flexible prices, allows an efficient allocation of productive effort, aggregating the needs of each individual.[9] In a nutshell, the argument is that we know better than the government our own needs and preferences.

To the Austrians' credit, in the 1930s and 1940s, there was nothing obvious about the idea that freedom was best for economic efficiency. Planning theories, in which the central government organizes production and decides on prices, had gained ground since World War I and ended up intellectually dominating after World War II. Planning had been successful at organizing war economies, and the Great Depression was blamed on a lack of government intervention. The Soviet model was attractive to many economists. It may come as a surprise today, but until 1989, one of the most widely used economics textbooks in the United States, *Economics* by Paul A. Samuelson and William D. Nordhaus, was quite positive about the planned economy and went as far as saying that "the Soviet economy is proof that, contrary to what many skeptics had previously believed, a managed socialist economy can work and even prosper."[10]

Sen: Freedom Is Valuable

A purely instrumental defense of freedom, however, ignores its intrinsic value. British economist John Hicks, in the late 1930s, was one of the few to note the strange amnesia of his colleagues. The positive contribution of freedom to economic efficiency should not be seen as its *raison d'être*: "The liberal, or non-interference, principles of the classical (Smithian or Ricardian) economists were not, in the first place, economic principles; they were an application to economics of principles that were thought to apply to a much wider field. The contention that economic freedom made for economic efficiency was no more than a secondary support.... What I do question is whether we are justified in forgetting, as completely as most of us have done, the other side of the argument."[11]

For instance, let us flip Hayek's argument on its head and imagine that a computer is powerful enough to make decisions that are the best for the economy. In such a case, what reason is there left to defend liberty? Should people not give up decision-making power to machines? As it turns out, this question is at the heart of Amartya Sen's work.

Sen is one of the few contemporary economists to emphasize the insufficient consideration of the value of freedom per se in economics. His famous example is not about powerful computers taking over our lives but about books and teachers. Even if the teacher knows which books we will like, we cherish the act of choosing for ourselves. Reading does not have the same flavor when it is forced upon us. Similarly, a chosen fast is not the same as an imposed one. In *Les Misérables*, nineteenth-century French novelist Victor Hugo highlights the intrinsic value of freedom with an example of this type: he compares the monastery and the prison, two places where men live confined in austere material conditions. From a strictly material point of view, the similarity between these two worlds is striking: "They are clothed in coarse woolen or coarse linen. Not one of them possesses in his own right anything whatever. . . . All undergo the same tonsure, wear the same frock, eat the same black bread, sleep on the same straw." But because it is chosen, the claustration of monks is of a radically different nature from that of the prisoners. It is lived as an ultimate act of freedom: "They do not come forth. By virtue of what right? By virtue of the right to go and come, which implies the right to remain at home. . . . Oh! how grand is liberty! And what a splendid transfiguration! Liberty suffices to transform the monastery into a republic."[12]

Amartya Sen had the project of integrating the intrinsic value of freedom into economic theory, but unfortunately this intellectual agenda did not gather a large following. One reason is that it would require changing how economists model decision-making. In the baseline economic model, agents derive utility from the actions (consumption, leisure, and so on) *they choose*, not the ones they *could have chosen*. But in order to account for liberty, the agent would also have to put value on the full range of possible actions, rather than the one path that was taken. For instance, assume Peter lives in New York City and likes classical music but never goes to the opera because he is too busy. Valuing potential consumption plans, not just realized ones, would explain why Peter would be happier to live in New York City than in Boston, which has no opera house: he has the *option* to go to the opera. Such a model would also help us understand the frustration generated by external constraints imposed on our choices, even when these do not influence the final result. For instance, some European governments tax their citizens at a higher rate than the United States but supply public goods in exchange (think: health care, unfunded pensions, transportation, child care, and so on). While, in the end, inhabitants of these countries may have the same consumption basket as, say, North Americans, some dimension of choice is taken away from them.[13]

Accounting for Freedom in Cost-Benefit Analysis

Despite Sen's continued warnings, recent developments in economic thought have continued to overlook the intrinsic value of freedom. Worse, since modern economics places no value on freedom, but people do, most policies will be biased toward restricting individual liberty too much.

Indeed, contemporary research has accumulated more and more evidence that agents, left to their own devices, fail to optimize welfare. This happens for essentially two reasons: *externalities* (our behavior can harm others) and *self-control* issues (we might do things that we will later regret). Externalities, such as pollution, can justify constraints on individual freedom to promote society's welfare. For instance, speed limits or traffic restrictions may be enforced to mitigate transportation risks and reduce air pollution. This is essentially economists' take on the limits of negative liberty: individual liberties that are harmful to others should be restricted. Meanwhile, self-control issues, involving situations where individuals may pose harm to themselves, have long been acknowledged as instances where coercive interventions are justified. For example, if someone is on the verge of jumping from a bridge due to a recent break-up, most would agree it is morally imperative to take action to prevent them from succeeding, even if force is required. In certain countries, the law even mandates it as a duty (for example, in France, failure to assist a person facing danger is considered a crime). In the same spirit, many paternalistic interventions limit individual choice—for instance, the requirement to wear a helmet while driving a motorcycle. Economists have pushed this logic further, involving less dramatic choices in our everyday life. This paternalism is their version of the philosophers' quest for positive liberty: economists believe that individuals sometimes make unwise choices. They want to help us all get closer to their ideal of utility maximization.

Both types of interventions can be effective, but they come at a cost that economic models neglect: the loss of some personal freedom.

Let us be clear here. We certainly do not reject the idea that public policies should deal with externalities and self-control problems. Economic research is perfectly right to point them out. But it often ignores that freedom has a price, and therefore that restricting it has a cost: economics fails to be explicit that there is a trade-off when it comes to suppressing some liberties.

While standard economic analysis ignores these trade-offs, society does not. Let's take an example: poor hygiene reduces the life expectancy of an individual and can be harmful (or at least unpleasant) for those who approach that person. On economic grounds, one could find it normal to impose a minimum number of showers per week. Some totalitarian regimes have indeed resorted to this. In the steppes of Mongolia, the communist regime used to carry out unannounced body examinations to inculcate in the nomads the habit of washing.[14] In our liberal societies, however, if hygiene inspections in restaurant kitchens seem legitimate, cleanliness inspections in our homes and on our bodies would clearly be considered too intrusive.

This illustration is so extreme that few people would disagree. Let us now explore situations in which there is more room for disagreement on whether public policies are too "liberticide" or not. The first debate we examine is freedom of speech; the second is the rise of "nudges" in everyday life promoted by behavioral economics.

How Much Should We Restrict Freedom of Expression?

The debate about freedom of expression on social media is a good example of the use of notions of externality and irrationality to limit freedom, with little regard for its intrinsic value. At the heart of this debate is the fashionable "echo chambers" theory. According to this theory, social media puts us in bubbles of like-minded people, and we are no longer exposed to contradiction. Legacy media's gate-keeping function is circumvented, allowing the proliferation of the most outlandish beliefs and the emergence of parallel narratives. This leads to *fake news* and conspiracies, reinforced by the famous "confirmation bias" described by psychologists (we neglect information that does not confirm our beliefs). Deprived of a common agora where theories are confronted, citizens, lost in the wilderness of the internet, become radicalized and polarized. An implicit conclusion of this theory is that freedom of expression must be rethought (understand: restricted). Resharing of content should be controlled. Anonymity should be limited. Posting should be restricted for some.

It is easy to see the limits of the argument. They are even too numerous to list exhaustively.[15] Echo chambers have always existed: newspapers, pub discussions, and political meetings have generated their fair share of radicalization. No contemporary media or Instagram influencer can rival the fear that Robespierre, one of the leaders of the French Revolution, had of *Le Vieux Cordelier*, the newspaper that spread the ideas of his political opponent Danton (this confrontation did not end well for either of them—they were both beheaded in 1794). The possibility to address a large audience is not new; the only difference is that it has been democratized beyond politicians, journalists, and professional intellectuals.

Another limitation of the echo chamber theory is that people are less naïve than academics think they are. They do not literally believe in the *fake news* they consume and diffuse; there is a gap between what is expressed and what is believed, like the gap between caricature and photography.[16] Several studies have explored the impact of Meta's algorithms, which feed users with content that is more likely to please them, during an election.[17] The echo chamber hypothesis is that these algorithms tend to aggravate political polarization in the population. However, the studies failed to detect such an effect. Yet, they were as close as it gets to the gold standard of modern social science. They divided Facebook and Instagram users into two groups, one of which received content delivered by Meta's usual algorithms, while the other received a news feed generated by simple chronological order. Those who received content chronologically spent less time on Meta's platforms and were exposed to more diverse content. But crucially there was no difference in the evolution of political polarization between the two groups.

But beyond the veracity of the echo chamber theory, the key issue here is that free speech has an intrinsic value. Even if the echo chamber theory were entirely true, restricting freedom of expression would not be costless. We all know the problems induced by limiting free speech: defining what can and what cannot be said, what is true and what is not, will eventually deteriorate trust in the media. Second, echo chamber theory lacks subtlety: rather than dismissing radical views out of hand, the role of the social scientist (professional or amateur) is to try and make them intelligible. Often, people do not mean exactly what they say, and it is up to the commentator to understand what they seek to express. A good example of such work is *Strangers in Their Own Land*, based on a series of interviews conducted by sociologist Arlie Russell Hochschild in Louisiana before the 2016 election.[18] She documented a deep distrust of environmental regulation, apparently at odds with complaints about the devastating impact of the oil industry on the Bayou. She also described how the positive effects of this industry were overestimated by the people she met. But instead of brushing off these attitudes as ill informed or incoherent, she tried to understand the moral concerns that they expressed (lack of fairness). Our bottom line here is that freedom of expression is precious because seemingly wrong or inconsistent affirmations often have a hidden meaning.

Illiberal Paternalism

Let us now move to a second theme, where we find modern economics erring on the side of restricting personal freedom a bit too quickly. Over the past few decades, the field of behavioral economics has accumulated a wealth of evidence of our predictable irrationalities and systematic errors of judgment. To the layperson, these findings will not sound as surprising as they did to economists. When trying to anticipate the future, we extrapolate too much from the recent past. We tend to give too much weight to our personal experiences instead of summoning all information freely available to us. We selectively forget past events, and when we do recall them, our memories are imperfect. We give in to our impulses and then regret it later. Finally, when it comes to important decisions about our future (such as savings choices or healthy lifestyle resolutions), we have an annoying tendency to procrastinate. All things that a proper *Homo economicus* would never do.

People would benefit a lot from getting rid of these biases. In economic terms, they would increase their utilities. Unfortunately, however, economists have found that education does not improve things much. For example, regarding making our savings decisions more rational, providing educational modules turns out to only have a limited impact (statistically significant and in the right direction, but small).[19] After all, it is not so surprising that education is not a panacea: it does not solve self-control problems. If I am prone to procrastination, being aware of it does not automatically help me.

Since it is difficult to convince people to change their behavior, even when it is harmful to them, the economist Richard Thaler and legal scholar Cass Sunstein have suggested an alternative solution: the *nudge*.[20] *Nudge* is a gentle form of manipulation to obtain the desired result. "Gentle" means noncoercive, and therefore compatible with the preservation of freedom. The most famous (though perhaps not the most tasteful) example of *nudge* is images of flies engraved in the urinals of certain airports, which lead men to aim better and improve toilet cleanliness. Another, more consequential example concerns retirement savings: in some American states, retirement savings are, by default, automatically invested in a well-managed, diversified fund, chosen by regulators. People can still decide to invest their retirement savings as they wish, but, and this is the trick, they have to *opt out* of the default option. This implies actively filling out forms and ticking boxes, and most people will not make that effort, mostly out of passivity. Generically, the intuition of *nudge* is to exploit our behavioral biases (impulse to drown the fly, passivity when it comes to managing our money) to induce irrational individuals to maximize their self-interest through the back door.

Nudge is intellectually attractive. It has the advantages of good old paternalism without concerns about (formal) freedom restrictions since individuals retain the right to do as they please. Since the publication of Thaler's book in 2008, many countries have embraced the idea with enthusiasm. These instances of *nudge* range from incentives to file taxes properly, to interventions to encourage barrier actions during the pandemic, to incentives to eat better, smoke less, sort waste, and so on. The most famous government unit applying these insights is the British Behavioural Insights Team, created in 2010, which was at one time directly advised by Thaler.

For all its useful insights (in particular, the notion that policy ergonomics are important), *nudge* comes at the cost of restricting our liberties. This cost tends to be ignored by its advocates, who are content with the preservation of formal freedom. But formal freedom is not real freedom. The *nudge* is designed by self-appointed "nudgelords"—as the statistician Andrew Gelman caustically calls them—who may not always be well intentioned or even competent.[21] Worse: the *nudge* is by design an invisible straitjacket, a stealth manipulation based on our impulse or passivity. Therefore, it prevents the individual from deliberating. It hinders the growth that comes from our agency.

A Thought Experiment

To get a feel for this problem, let us undertake a small thought experiment—a caricature of the *nudge* idea. We know that one of the main problems of modern democracies is abstention. To solve this problem, imagine a clever behavioral economist proposes the following reform: by default, our ballot would be cast with the name of a candidate chosen by a committee staffed by competent experts. Their choice would likely go for a moderate, technocratic candidate, with good pedagogical skills. This option saves most voters the trouble of going to the polls and even comparing programs; it gently nudges them to vote for the "right candidate." Those who don't agree with the committee can always go to the polls, the old-fashioned way. They remain free to vote for whomever they like. If the disciples of *nudge* have not yet dared to propose this mechanism, it is because it is an offense to our democratic instinct (and hopefully theirs). It demotivates collective reflection on political issues. It stifles deliberation and the production of legitimacy. Citizens are discouraged from forming their own judgments, debating, and accepting the outcome of the collective debate. There is of course also a risk of confiscation of power by the committee of "nudgelords."

Do People Want to Be Nudged?

This criticism of *nudge* would be moot if people did willingly consent to be nudged. To go back to our caricatural example above, it would be harder to criticize the "ballot by default" approach if voters had explicitly consented (via referendum, for instance) to this rule under the veil of ignorance—that is, long before the default candidate was chosen. Inspired by this remark, we investigated the acceptance of *nudge* in our survey of US residents, through the following (admittedly less drastic) thought experiment:

> American adults eat too much sugar. This causes illnesses and deaths. As a result, some advocate measures to limit the purchase of foods that are high in sugar.
>
> A proposed regulation works like this. In supermarkets, sweet snacks, candies, and sodas would have to be stored in a special cabinet with a locked glass door. Customers passing by the cabinet would get a text message with a 25-digit code. They could then open the cabinet by punching in this 25-digit code. This task would not take more than a minute. Once the cabinet is open, customers can purchase whatever they want.
>
> How much do you agree with this new regulation?

This hypothetical describes a regulation in the spirit of *nudge*, which is designed to discourage impulse purchases of sweet snacks but does not make them at all impossible. If people were worried about their self-control problems, they should welcome this solution as a cheap, noninvasive way of dealing with them.

Yet, our US survey participants strongly reject it: 81 percent disagree with the proposal. Attitude toward *nudge* does not seem to be explained by political leaning: the rejection rate is 79 percent for liberals, and 83 percent for conservatives. Participants do not reject the *nudge* out of insensitivity to public health concerns. In the cross-section, the attitude to *nudge* does not correlate with empathy, as measured by the "compassion" question described at the beginning of chapter 2. Of course, a lot more analysis would be needed, for instance, by suggesting different *nudges*. Also, one explanation of our findings could be that participants underestimate the effect of excess sugar consumption on welfare (of themselves, of others). The design of this question can be fixed to take this into account.

Taking Stock

In economics, freedom is most often seen as a means to an end rather than an intrinsic good. Its usefulness lies in optimally allocating resources and stimulating entrepreneurship and innovation. It is also a way to allow individuals, who know best what is good for them, to further their own interests.

However, when individuals hurt themselves by acting irrationally or hurt others via externalities, freedom is considered by economists as harmful. This leads to a variety of (justified) prescriptions to modify individual behaviors. But the problem is that these prescriptions do not account for the intrinsic value of liberty.

We believe this trend is not without dangers. It could lead to a loss of pluralism, excessive normalization of social behavior, and imposition of the majority's will. Nonconformism also has positive externalities on society, the first one being creativity. Sanitizing personal decisions, penalizing eccentricity, stigmatizing unconventional behaviors: the perils of this type of project are amply demonstrated by history. Precisely because they make us distinct from utility-maximizing robots, some of the messy and erratic aspects of human behavior should be cherished and valued rather than eliminated.

While freedom should have limits, these limits should be drawn by carefully balancing the utilitarian benefits of restrictions and the cost that losing the freedom to choose entails for both the individual and society. This "price of freedom" should be carefully measured by investigating the population's preferences rather than determined by the technocratic apparatus of government.

4
Markets and Communities

In the public debate, economists are prompt to denounce the lack of competition between companies and, more broadly, any sort of acquired privilege or status that individuals might benefit from (for instance, civil servants or railway workers). They call them "rents," a pejorative term that suggests an undeserved reward (one might recall John Maynard Keynes advocating for the "euthanasia of the rentier").[1] Recently, a major concern in US policy circles has been that eroding competition has been a cause of sluggish growth. "Fair competition is why capitalism has been the world's greatest force for prosperity and growth," Joe Biden said on July 9, 2021.[2] In that speech, the US president praised the strength of President Franklin D. Roosevelt's antitrust enforcement, which, he said, "help[ed] set the course for sustained economic growth after World War II." To unlock growth, a traditional prescription is to toughen competition by enforcing antitrust regulation that punishes cartels and by facilitating firms' entry such that entrepreneurs can more easily "disrupt" existing businesses. In the United States, the Antitrust Division of the Department of Justice and the Federal Trade Commission enforce antitrust policies. Their mission is to prevent firms from extracting abnormally high prices from consumers.

This view of the positive consequences of high competition is based on the "first welfare theorem." In a nutshell, the logic is this: when they have few competitors, companies take into account the fact that producing more reduces consumers' appetite and therefore lowers sales prices. To prevent this from happening, they refrain from producing and make the economy poorer.

Competition is popular on the left not only because it increases total production but also because it guarantees a form of fairness and redistribution: more competition means transferring wealth from the rich to the poor, from shareholders to consumers, from idle old "rentiers" to deserving young entrepreneurs. Competition inherently rewards the deserving and promotes equal opportunities. What's not to like about that?

This chapter argues, mostly using insights from sociology, that there is also a dark side to competition. Rents can be the glue of society. Eliminating them can dangerously stress the social fabric. Our goal here is to highlight this cost, which tends to be ignored but should be factored in by public policy (the "optimal" level of competition may be lower than economists think).

Economic Defense of Rents

Before taking a sociological and psychological look at the role of rents in our societies, let us begin by clearing up a common misunderstanding: economic theory, properly understood, does not say that rents are always toxic. It does not advocate for implementing perfect competition. The reason is the dynamics involved in the productive process: firms or entrepreneurs need to first sink in initial investments (invent new products, set up production facilities) and then compete to sell their products. The prospect of rents in the second stage encourages firms to invest in the first place. Market power—that is, the ability to sell a good for more than it costs to produce it—is the catalyst of innovation. Some of our institutions are based on this idea. Patents, for example, enable temporary monopolies, ensuring that investors can reap significant profits from their discoveries. This legal right to monopolize a technology for a limited duration acts as a positive incentive for seeking patentable innovations. Such rewards for invention are crucial in sectors with high innovation costs, like the pharmaceutical sector.

When Economic Efficiency Dehumanizes: Durkheimian Anomie

Sociologists have long voiced a different critique of competition. According to them, it promotes selfish behavior, thereby damaging the cooperation essential to a harmonious social life. In the following discussion, we will explore the various aspects of this sociological attack on competition.

One of the pioneers of this critique is Émile Durkheim, the French sociologist whom we introduced in chapter 2. In the second preface of *The Division of Labor in Society*, published in 1893, Durkheim famously theorized that the relentless pursuit of economic efficiency accompanying industrialization could be mentally draining for individuals, depriving them of important aspects of a fulfilling life at work. In the fierce Darwinian race for survival that competition imposes, traditional workplaces are driven out of business. The fittest companies are not those that contribute to the quality of life and the flourishing of their employees. They are those that optimize efficiency by increasing worker specialization. The modern employee becomes a cog in the machine, endlessly repeating the same tasks over and over, as in Charlie Chaplin's movie *Modern Times*. In the name of efficiency, work is stripped of its purpose. Relations between colleagues are reduced to the bare minimum.

Durkheim was deeply concerned with the "anomie" (normlessness) resulting from the growing influence of industry on society to the detriment of local solidarity and cooperation. Like Montesquieu and Tocqueville before him, he feared the advent of a society of atomized individuals, lacking the support of well-structured communities, defenseless against the power of the state: "A society composed of an infinite dust of unorganized individuals, which a hypertrophied State strives to enclose and retain, constitutes a true sociological monstrosity."[3]

Durkheim thought corporatism could be a solution. The corporation defines collective norms and rituals, a framework that provides insertion into a community at a human scale and that helps define a full career path. The members of a corporation do not compete for jobs, for customers: they cooperate but also exchange and socialize. The prose of the founder of modern sociology, usually analytical and rigorous, becomes lyrical when evoking the benefits of corporatism: "A group is not only a moral authority, it is also a source of life sui generis. From it emanates a warmth that warms and revives hearts, that opens them to sympathy, that melts selfishness."[4]

On the other side of the Rhine, Max Weber shared the same pessimistic assessment of industrial society, captured by the "iron cage" metaphor. He coined the term in the last pages of his famous work *The Protestant Ethic and the Spirit of Capitalism*, published in 1904. At its foundation, capitalism was powered by the quest for God's approval. But its spirit has been perverted by modernity. The objective of economic agents is no longer to learn if they are chosen, if they have God's grace. It has become "the pursuit of wealth, stripped of its religious and ethical meaning." "The Puritan wanted to work in a calling; we are forced to do so."[5] By chaining us to our self-interest, modernity has stripped us of our free will and made us prisoners of the iron cage.

Market Overdose Dries Up the Soul

For Durkheim, competition does not only make us cogs of the economic machine; it also dries up our souls. According to him, competition forces each one of us to think of ourselves as besieged soldiers, threatened by others. Nothing can be taken for granted. Sellers cannot count on the loyalty or forgiveness of their customers—they are engaged in a perpetual battle to be chosen. Workers are also continuously put on the spot, needing to convince their employers that they are the best at their job, that there is no better alternative to them in the labor market. This state of mind invites people to avoid cooperation. They lose their ability to care for others: "If, in the occupations that fill almost all our time, we follow no other rule than that of our own self-interest, how will we acquire a taste for selflessness, self-forgetfulness and sacrifice?"[6]

Following Durkheim's footsteps, sociologist Arlie Russell Hochschild also thinks that too much market can damage—rather than dry up—the soul. One of her key arguments is that the modern labor market invades our inner selves, our private lives; it robs us of our personal experiences. Her starting point is the rise of personal services jobs in the postindustrial society. Many of these new jobs entail what Hochschild calls "emotional labor," that is, work that involves not only physical and mental tasks but also the provision of empathy. These jobs include child and senior care, nursing, hospitality, retail, and so on. Renting out one's emotions can be more alienating than simply renting out one's strength or brain because emotions are not something that can be switched on and off at will. Eventually, work takes over, and people become their professional selves all day long. It changes their identities.[7] The rise of personal services also hurts customers. We are all amateurs in our private lives. For many of the things we do for our friends and family (child care, education, and so forth), we ourselves have no expertise. The market supplies the services of professionals who have extensive experience and training. They take care of our children better, they can organize better vacations, plan our weddings, and so on. We owe it to our loved ones, to ourselves, to go for the superior market alternative. In this way, competition from the market deprives us of our private lives.[8]

In economics, a small neo-Durkheimian literature develops these sociological intuitions by studying how the predominance of the market dehumanizes behavior. This line of research shows that competition at all costs (which guarantees the absence of rents) puts individuals in "survival mode." Ethics are a luxury that is affordable only when one's own survival is guaranteed, but competition posits that survival should never be taken for granted. A second insight from this literature is that the market tones down moral feelings because it relieves us of our responsibilities. Focused on the abstract accounting of costs and benefits, individuals become emotionally disconnected from the consequences of their actions. Placed in a market situation, they behave like athletes in a sports competition. They score as many points as they can, regardless of their sympathy for their competitors. In a series of experiments, the economists Armin Falk, Nora Szech, and colleagues show that competitive situations lead participants to optimize their financial interests, coldly forgetting ethics.[9] They propose a theory based on the dilution of responsibilities: in a competitive market, we see the price of things not as depending on us but as the result of market interactions. No one feels responsible, like the soldiers in a firing squad who can plausibly deny (to themselves, to others) having fired the fatal bullet. It makes us insensitive to harm caused (to mice in their experiments).

This suggests that introducing the market into a domain from which it was previously absent leads to changes in the behavior of the actors within that domain. In this scenario, individuals tend to set aside their altruistic inclinations. A famous experiment illustrates this: Uri Gneezy and Aldo Rustichini studied the response of parents to the introduction (in an Israeli daycare center) of a fixed fine when parents picked up their children after the official closing time.[10] Instead of reducing tardiness, as one might have hoped, the fine increased it. It broke the implicit convention of doing everything possible to be on time. Paying a fine frees one from a social norm and grants a right: one can now legitimately be late since one is paying for it. The fine has transformed the violation of a rule into a legitimate cash transaction.

Investing in Social Capital to Grow the Community

Another reason why the market can be toxic to society is that rents are what holds the community together. The broad argument is that communities thrive on the investment of their members (what sociologists call "social capital"), and the payback comes in the form of rents. Attack these rents (through competition), and the community will become weaker. This is the view articulated by the economist Raghuram Rajan in his book *The Third Pillar*.[11] It may sound a bit abstract, but it is in fact very concrete. Let us explain.

To build intuition, let us start with the workplace (which is a form of community). In many firms, senior employees or suppliers benefit from rents. They have been around for a while, their skills are dated, and they are well paid. Some of them could be replaced by younger, better, more effective alternatives. The spread between how much they receive and what competitors would pay is a rent. In some countries, employees with seniority are more costly to fire, effectively forcing firms to keep them on the payroll even though the labor market offers better alternatives. In the United States, public sector employees enjoy strong job security. Even in private universities, professors are provided with tenure if they have been successful at publishing and teaching during their tenure track (which typically lasts about six years). Partnerships in law firms or asset management companies also provide certain rights that can be perceived as rents. Overall, once people obtain them, these rents look like favoritism.

Yet, these rents are there for a reason. Throughout their careers, employees contribute to growing the institution they work for. They develop part of its "intangible" capital: its organization, language, internal processes, and information system. These are all elements of the corporate culture that are progressively built by employees. Sales representatives establish the reputation of the firm. Engineers and researchers improve the production process, invent new products. When employees leave the company, these investments stay on and benefit its owners. The prospect of being better paid in the future is an incentive mechanism: I invest today, the company will keep me as an employee, and it will pay me better in the future. As in the pharmaceutical example, rents might seem useless *after the fact*, but cutting them would discourage investment a priori. The same logic applies to other stakeholders: suppliers, local community, and so on.

Of course, companies could try to make promises to their employees (invest in me, I will pay you back), but promises are fragile. Once a company has "cashed in" on its workers' investments, it will be tempted to betray its word. A familiar example of this is in corporate acquisitions: when "raiders" takes control of a company through a hostile takeover, they can be tempted to break implicit agreements made by the previous owner (like not firing employees nearing retirement or being loyal to certain suppliers). Such a breach of trust benefits the new owner but comes at the expense of other stakeholders, eroding trust.[12] For instance, new employees may understandably become wary of believing the promises of the new owner. Moreover, this distrust can extend to other companies as everyone fears being exposed to similar opportunistic behavior. So, in this example, market forces might seem efficient (the new owner might brag about increasing productivity), but in reality, they erode the motivation of economic agents.

This intuition, coming from financial economics, extends to investment in building a thriving community, in accumulating "social capital." The market hurts the community because it constantly gives its members an opportunity to check if there is a better alternative elsewhere. If there is, agents will stop investing in the community, draining its life.

Economist Eli Berman illustrates this insight in the case of Ultra-Orthodox communities in Israel.[13] Imagine a vibrant community of religious people who value active discussions of Torah and participation in communal activities at synagogues. This intense religious atmosphere demands significant commitment from its members, requiring many hours per day dedicated to studying religion and preparing for community events. But such a high level of commitment conflicts with full-time paid employment. Individually, each member desires both a well-paying job and the benefits of community life. When the job market becomes too attractive, the community unravels. The temptation of higher wages proves irresistible, leading everyone to prioritize paid labor over community engagement. This cycle of events is a Durkheimian doom loop: the presence of the labor market weakens the community's cohesion. To prevent it, the community may just try to reduce its members' access to the labor market. This is Berman's theory for why some Orthodox Jews do not learn marketable skills at school. This ensures that they will remain committed to the group, and at some point, it will be too late to go back to school. While this will seem to many a big breach of individual autonomy, there is a clear benefit: a lively community.[14]

There are many examples where markets can diminish some nonmonetary contributions crucial for social functioning. For instance, Henrik Cronqvist and his coauthors conducted a study on the impact of subsidies for crop insurance introduced in the 1980s, compensating US farmers for poor crop yields.[15] Farmers started to use the insurance market. Using financial contracts weakened the need for local solidarity, which decreased religious practice in counties where insurance contracts were introduced. Both religious adherence and the size of church congregations decreased, illustrating how financial markets can negatively affect communal activities' strength. In a similar vein, Gustav Agneman and Esther Chevrot-Bianco found that, in Greenland villages where the market economy is more present (they measure in each village whether local people use a formal labor and food market), villagers exhibit universalist moral behavior, treating villagers and nonvillagers alike. On the other hand, in villages relying on informal economic relationships (such as exchanging food locally), villagers demonstrate stronger solidarity toward fellow villagers compared to strangers.[16] This further highlights the impact of financial markets on the dynamics of communal interactions.

Neighborhoods: Collective Success Stories

This insight (that rents can be good for society) also applies to the housing market. In local neighborhoods, residents have an impact on housing prices through their investments in communal life. Economists like to describe the high house prices in the most attractive neighborhoods as resulting from artificial scarcity. They typically suggest that building new homes could address this issue. While this perspective holds some truth, it overlooks the fact that elevated house prices can also result from the genuine investment of community members. It takes many hours of town hall meetings to learn the ropes of local politics, whether the town really needs a budget override or not or whether to build a new library or a new hockey rink. Disgruntled parents need to run for the school board to push for changes in their children's education.

Residents spend time tending their gardens, renovating their houses, and organizing community events that make the neighborhood a collective success story. As other people are interested in joining the neighborhood, housing prices go up. Make these gains disappear (through taxation or building additional housing), and you will have reduced individual incentives to build the community.

The Glue of Society

The "retail apocalypse" is a stark example of competition hurting communities. Over the years, economists have tirelessly advocated that policies should facilitate the creation of supermarkets to boost employment.[17] More recently, the development of e-commerce has been celebrated as a gain in efficiency. When you only look at the financial benefits, it is clear that the disappearance of small shops in town centers is more than compensated by the gains of the consumer and the creation of jobs in big stores.

The problem with this cost-benefit analysis is that it fails to consider the social impact induced by retail business: a lively city center facilitates local human interactions, increases foot traffic and public safety, and allows elderly people without cars to stay in town. The presence of shops further influences real estate prices through these channels and also contributes to social capital, a source of trust and cooperation in the community. The suburban supermarket does not replace any of these social contributions. In the end, competition in retail destroys social capital, which may be more valuable to local residents than the opportunity of buying goods at lower prices.

A report written for the French government after the Yellow Vest movement finds evidence consistent with this. There is a statistical link between the disappearance of downtown small businesses, the feeling of abandonment expressed by France's small cities, and the protests that took over the country in the fall of 2018.[18]

Before the 1960s, competition policy seemed mindful of these effects. Sociologist Elizabeth Popp Berman shows that, before antitrust became solely focused on maximizing economic efficiency, regulators had the additional goals of protecting small businesses, preserving the geographic balance of economic activity across the United States, and preventing the excessive concentration of power in the hands of a few individuals.[19] Interestingly, the paradigm that prevailed was somewhat informal (compared to what economic analysis allows) but more open than the narrow focus on consumer welfare that came to prevail in the late 1960s. For instance, the economic argument that larger firms can generate more consumer welfare if they are more efficient started to gain ground during this period—whether due to the rising influence of the Chicago school or to intense lobbying by big business.[20] Until then, making sure firms remained small was an explicit objective of competition policy, in order to preserve local communities.

Rents at the Absolute Zero: An Unlivable World

Let us add a final Durkheimian argument to this defense of rents. It applies to corporate rents and is based on risk. Imagine rents are at "absolute zero," a hypothetical situation where everyone benefits, as a consumer, from extreme competition between firms and between workers. In this fictitious economy, rents are nonexistent. Companies are barely profitable. As a result, as soon as a firm becomes temporarily less productive than its competitors, its profits turn into losses. The firm needs to fire its workers and temporarily shut down. In this thought experiment, all this is perfectly efficient. More productive firms immediately hire back the workers who were just fired, and the entrepreneur finds another occupation. But this theoretical world is only viable in a perfectly fluid and mobile economy, that of mathematical models. In the real world, with its frictions (firms cannot "temporarily" shut down, migrating is difficult, it takes time to find a job, and so on), rents (in this example, positive profits) are a positive thing because they provide insurance to companies and employees. These economic rents are buffers that give people time to turn around when the going gets tough.

The bottom line is that rents offer some insurance. They reduce the amount of uncertainty that economic agents (entrepreneurs, workers) have to bear, at the cost of some economic inefficiency. But why use corporate rents to insure workers? Isn't it inefficient? One could imagine a world where people could pool these risks with one another, and the lucky could pay off the unfortunate, as in car insurance. Everyone is paid. If this sounds like economic fiction, it is simply because it is. In the real world, such insurance most often does not exist. Think, for instance, about insurance against the risk that one's job is destroyed by technological change—or that one's neighborhood becomes dangerous and that house prices fall.

Good Rents, Bad Rents

Let us be clear. We do not mean to say all rents should be maintained and untouched. Certain privileges can make the economy, and even society, sclerotic: there is a balance to be found between rents and openness to market forces. On several occasions, we ourselves have publicly taken positions in favor of entrants in markets that were suffering from a pathological lack of competition, such as telecoms or ridesharing. In these situations, the rents of incumbent firms were clear, and the service they provided was less than ideal.

Our goal in this chapter has been to show that some rents are vital to society, as they are vital to innovation. Economists tend to criticize them in the public debate, without considering social or human subtleties. This implicit social Darwinism, even dressed up in the garb of equal opportunity and meritocracy, increases the amount of stress in society. In a perfectly competitive world, we would all be on an ejector seat, summoned to prove we are always, every day, "the best person for the job," "the best resident of this neighborhood," or "the best user of this wealth." Permanently on the go, we should always move where we are the most useful, to the detriment of long-term relationships and investment in social capital. The danger is for people to become atoms, mere cogs in the machine of competition and efficiency.

Cutting blindly into rents with the conviction of building a better world is naïve. Some rents are unfair and inefficient, but many of them are here for a reason. We think it is important to approach the issue of rents from this broader perspective. One way to do this is to investigate and take on board people's opinions: people are intuitive social scientists whose views are legitimate and often informed. They think not just as economists but also as intuitive psychologists, philosophers, and sociologists. That they are not experts can be a strength, for it allows them to see the bigger picture. So at this point let us turn to our survey.

Distorting Competition to Preserve the Local Community

We have asked our survey participants for their views on a tax designed to support city-center stores. The cost borne by residents varies from 10 to 50 to 100 euros/dollars (each participant is randomly assigned one of these tax increases). Furthermore, for half of the participants, the decision comes from the mayor, and for the other half, it comes from the central government. This question is part of our survey run in the United States, France, and Germany.

> You live in a small town. To preserve the life of the downtown area where small businesses are struggling, [the mayor/government] proposes to reduce their taxes. This will allow merchants to maintain their business. This measure will be financed by an increase in your [local/national] taxes of about [10/50/100] euros/dollars per year.
>
> Do you agree with this decision [of the mayor/government]? Rate from 1 to 10, where 1 means you strongly disagree and 10 means you strongly agree.

The first salient point is that participants are in favor of distorting competition, but to a limited extent. Results are quite sensitive to taxes. When raising the cost of this intervention from 10 to 100 dollars in the United States, the average answer drops from 6.5 (strong support) to 5.5 (more lukewarm). In France, the drop is much larger, from 6.5 to 4.5

(leaning toward rejection), presumably because the level of taxation is higher in Europe already. A second important point is who decides matters in building legitimacy. Support is on average about 0.5 larger when the decision comes from the mayor than when it comes from the central government. Unsurprisingly, in these very local matters, people want to be in the loop.

Who is willing to bend the rules of competition to preserve the community? Interestingly, these participants are equally likely to be conservatives or progressives. There is, however, a difference between participants who express strong *collectivist* values and *individualists*. To build this measure of collectivism/individualism, we use answers to four questions from the Moral Foundations Questionnaire designed by Jonathan Haidt and his coauthors.[21] These four questions describe each person's adherence to the moral values of fairness, compassion, authority, and loyalty to the in-group.[22] We label people who score high on all values "collectivists": they think the will of the individual should be subordinated to society. People who score low on all values are in contrast labeled "individualists": they believe in the sanctity of individual autonomy, freedom from authority, loyalty to the group, rules of fairness, and duties to care about others. In our survey, these "rugged individualists"—who can be found on both sides of the political spectrum—are more likely to support free competition and to be hostile to subsidizing small stores. Interestingly, we also found that collectivists are more likely to support protectionism to uphold moral values or industrial policy that favors local production over imported train equipment. These results are reminiscent of the sociology of Durkheim. Our "collectivist" participants would agree with him about the virtues of a community and the need to protect it from the destructive forces of competition.[23]

Antitrust Should Take Social Externalities into Account

The overarching message of this book is that one cannot separate economics from morals. In this chapter, we have argued that competition not only affects the degree of efficiency of the economy but may also have psychological and sociological effects. Competition does not stand in a vacuum; it takes place in a society with real people, and it has moral implications. As a result, competition policy should not only focus on consumer welfare (optimizing the material consumption of economic agents) but also account for social externalities.

Of course, competition has many positive aspects. It improves economic efficiency—except when it discourages investment in innovation. It is meritocratic—it rewards the most efficient and the most hardworking. It is compatible with individual liberties. As academic researchers, we are keenly aware of the merits of competition in the production of ideas.

But at the same time, we can multiply examples of what seem to be necessary distortions to the principle of perfect competition. The Jeffersonian intuition that small firms should be preserved as part of the fabric of society is sound. Anyone who has visited deserted city centers in the United States or Europe can easily conceive that small businesses have a positive social function in urban centers. Their disappearance has accelerated the disaggregation of communal life. The health of the economy presupposes a healthy distribution over the whole territory. National champions in arms and technology may be needed for a nation to remain sovereign.

These considerations, which are somewhat qualitative in nature, used to be better taken into account. This was before the exclusive consideration of consumer welfare, dictated by economic models, became the regulators' sole compass. It is therefore undoubtedly necessary to reintegrate considerations of social externalities into the decision criteria and the thinking of the regulators. This will require surveys that directly elicit the preferences of people: what they value in their life, what they find fair, what they are anxious about. It will require better bridges between sociology and economics, so that our models better integrate what makes communities thrive beyond the build-up of individual wealth.

5
Justice

How much are we willing to sacrifice to live in a just world? Most economists would formulate this question as a tension between equality and efficiency. Conservative economists argue that reducing inequality harms the economy. Taxing the rich, they say, deters the creation of jobs and new businesses. Taxes discourage people from working or investing. Progressive economists counter that these incentive effects surely exist, but that they are quantitatively small: it should be cheap to make the world more equal.

In the population, the notion of fairness is less focused on inequality—it has many facets. To describe this diversity, the Norwegian economists Alexander Cappelen and Bertil Tungodden speak about "fairness pluralism."[1] Some people (call them libertarians) think that individuals or families naturally own the fruit of their labor. According to their view, taxation is akin to theft, and inequality is just, as long as it does not rely on expropriation. On the other side, strict egalitarians argue that no amount of inequality is legitimate, even if it helps the economy. In the middle, meritocrats think that people who work harder deserve more. They view equality as unfair when it does not reward merit.

In this chapter, we will delve into these intricacies. We use several examples to highlight the subtleties of fairness criteria that people use and that can be considered moral. Let us start with higher education.

SFFA v. Harvard

A good example of the ambiguity of what people perceive as fair or not is the lawsuit brought by a group of students against Harvard University. Harvard's prestige cannot be overstated. It has trained eight American presidents and four of the nine current Supreme Court justices. No fewer than 161 Nobel laureates teach or have taught there. In 2021, its endowment was worth more than $50 billion. Not surprisingly, Harvard is the university that attracts the most ambitious high schoolers (it admits only about 1,600 per year). Faced with this enormous demand, the admissions office is under constant scrutiny, since it defines who wins and who loses in the great game of American meritocracy.

Some believe its decisions are unjust. On November 17, 2014, Students for Fair Admissions (SFFA), an organization mostly representing Asian students, filed a complaint against the university for discrimination. What followed was one of those legal thrillers America is famous for: district court ruling in 2019, appeal in 2020, and Supreme Court decision in 2023.

The plaintiffs' expert, Peter Arcidiacono, a professor at Duke University, shows that, given their grades (high school GPA and SAT scores), Asian students are penalized compared to other ethnic groups. For a student of Asian descent who would have a 25 percent probability of being admitted (thus a good student), a white student with the same record would have a 36 percent probability of being admitted, a Hispanic student would have a 77 percent probability, and an African American student would have a 95 percent probability of admission.[2] Using data made available by the university, Arcidiacono also showed that "personality" scores, an eminently subjective assessment made by the admissions office based on the student's file alone, were systematically lower for Asian applicants. Yet the expert notes that Asian applicants' actual interview scores are not lower than those of other applicants. In other words, despite having much better academic records, many Asian applicants were rejected by Harvard, in part because of a subjective assessment given by staff members who had not even spoken to them.

Despite this strong case, lower court judges at first dismissed the plaintiffs. To summarize, the basis for these court decisions rests on jurisprudence from earlier cases (the main ones being Supreme Court decisions from 1978, 2003, and 2013). These rulings essentially established that race could be used in admissions as long as (1) it helps increase diversity on campus and (2) it is one of many factors in a holistic admissions process. Judges sided with Harvard on the basis that, as long as the university follows this rule, it has the right to freely define how it promotes diversity (a logic that comes from the First Amendment to the US Constitution, which guarantees, among other things, academic freedom). The objective of diversity is legally important because it is a "compelling interest" that allows bypassing the equal protection clause of the Fourteenth Amendment (which guarantees the equal treatment of all US citizens, irrespective of race). A problem, of course, is that diversity has many dimensions: race, but also parental income, religious affiliation, political leanings, and so on. If universities wanted students to be perfectly representative of the general population, the only option for them would be to draw a random sample of applicants, and therefore give up on their right to screen them. This internal contradiction of the diversity argument weakens the case for race-conscious admission, despite current jurisprudence. The Supreme Court was, indeed, aware of this limitation, stating in a 2003 opinion that "25 years from now, the use of racial preferences will no longer be necessary."[3]

Given these weaknesses, SFFA took the case to the Supreme Court. The parties were heard on October 31, 2022.[4] The plaintiffs argued that race is not just a "plus" in admissions (which would make race-conscious admissions acceptable) but a "predominant factor" since the racial composition of admitted students can be shown to be stable from one year to the next. Another argument of the plaintiffs is that discrimination against Asian Americans was intentional (which violates the equal protection clause of the Fourteenth Amendment). Evidence of this is the lower personality rating of Asian candidates, in spite of them doing well at interviews. Overall SFFA highlights the claim that trying to achieve racial diversity is unfair to Asian Americans.

The Supreme Court ruled on June 29, 2023, that Harvard's admission approach breached the equal protection clause, as it was found to discriminate against Asian American applicants. This decision overturns the previous rulings of lower courts. It applies to all colleges and universities. But it leaves them free to consider nonacademic factors other than race in the admissions process, such as socioeconomic status, geographic location, extracurricular activities, or even a student's account of how their race has shaped their experiences. Thus, it is not yet clear how the ruling will affect final admission outcomes. While confirming it will comply with the law, Harvard has stated that it strongly believes diversity is essential to academic excellence.

The legal dispute exposes the tension between two perspectives on fairness: equal representation of all races versus fair treatment of academic merit. This tension comes from the fact that it is impossible to achieve both objectives at the same time because, in the US population, race is correlated with academic achievement. This makes it physically impossible for universities to reflect the racial composition of the country, while at the same time imposing the same academic standards on everyone. The oral arguments presented by SFFA before the Supreme Court reflect this impossible dilemma. At one point, the discussion revolves around the idea that university admissions are a "zero-sum game"—that admitting an extra student from an underrepresented minority (URM, in higher education jargon) will force the university to reject a deserving nonminority applicant. The least compelling case made by Harvard's lawyers at that point is to deny the existence of such a trade-off.

Is Meritocracy an Absolute?

In this legal battle, two notions of justice are in opposition. Universities lean on the Civil Rights Act and jurisprudence to advocate for *equality of conditions*. The plaintiffs stand for *equality of opportunity*, that is, for meritocracy. As we will argue, however, most people balance a mixture of both views.

Meritocracy has a strong popular basis in the United States. According to a 2022 Pew Research Center survey, 61 percent of Americans think that high school grades should be a major factor in college admissions, while only 7 percent think that race should be a major factor for admissions.[5] A nuance to this picture is that Americans also tend to agree with some sort of holistic assessment of merit. Nineteen percent think community involvement should be a major factor (48 percent think it should be a minor one). Thirty-six percent of the participants tend to agree with some weight for athletic ability. Overall, participants mostly agree with the primacy of academic merit, but many also want to reward other types of achievements.

The other salient fact coming from the Pew survey is that, while people on average agree with meritocratic objectives, they are not "absolutists." For example, a large minority, 46 percent, agrees with the idea of giving an edge to first-generation applicants (making this a "minor" or even a "major" factor of admission). And most colleges do this.

We need to address the elephant in the room. Besides giving some priority to first-gen students, many colleges also give priority to children of faculty and alumni. This policy of "legacy admissions" contradicts the logic of equality of opportunity. It is not as popular as the strict meritocratic rule, but 25 percent of the Pew survey participants do actually agree with some preference for "legacy" students. One possibility is that these participants think of universities as a kind of club, whose goal is not only to educate but also to nurture a community. Another potential explanation for the nonzero support for legacy admissions is that legacy students are on average wealthier and thus indirectly subsidize poorer students through family donations or by paying full tuition.

To test more directly whether people are willing to compromise on meritocracy, we asked our own US survey participants to consider the following hypothetical proposal:

> The cost of attending college is very high in the US. Imagine that a group of well-known universities makes the following proposal:
>
> - For most students, these costs would be dramatically reduced. These students would be admitted on the basis of academic merit.
> - An extra 5% of spots would be sold by colleges to the highest bidder. Students who bid the highest price would thus be admitted, irrespective of their academic merit.
>
> Revenues generated by the sale of these extra spots would cover the reduced tuition of students admitted on the basis of academic merit.
>
> How much do you support this proposal?

Remember that our survey is run on a representative sample of 939 US residents. As in the Pew survey, most people are no meritocracy-absolutists. Forty-seven percent of the participants agree (somewhat or strongly) with the proposal to auction a few admission spots to the highest bidders.

Note that this question just pits two different views of fairness against one another. It does not elicit the intensity with which participants care about justice *in general*. In the same survey, we asked respondents whether they think that "it is morally wrong that rich children inherit a lot of money while poor children inherit nothing." We find essentially no correlation between support for our proposal and the answer to this question. Participants who are willing to auction off admission slots are *not* more, or less, tolerant of inherited inequality per se.

Rewarding Merit Can Be Unfair

Thus, most people are not "pure" meritocrats. The reason is not that their moral compass is impaired but rather that pure meritocracy, as an ideal, does not come without moral drawbacks.

The first criticism of meritocracy is simply that abilities (whether they come from the genetic lottery or childhood conditions) are neither equal nor something under our control. Pure meritocracy in education (as advocated by SFFA) is *efficient*: it selects the best students. But it is not *fair* because the winners have had a head start, so the others are not given a fair chance to win. This insight was famously expressed in President Lyndon B. Johnson's commencement speech at Howard University in 1965, just after the Civil Rights Act enshrined equal treatment of citizens into law:[6]

> Thus, it is not enough just to open the gates of opportunity. All our citizens must have the ability to walk through those gates.
>
> This is the next and the more profound stage of the battle for civil rights. We seek not just freedom but opportunity. We seek not just legal equity but human ability, not just equality as a right and a theory but equality as a fact and equality as a result.

This speech is often said to have started the spread of affirmative action policies in federal agencies. The logic is simple: if we want to achieve equality of conditions, we cannot just rely on equality of opportunity. We need to help those who are the most disadvantaged in their abilities and circumstances.

How to Reconcile Meritocracy with Equality of Conditions

To reconcile meritocracy with equality of conditions, one avenue to explore is the following: society's rewards, such as university admissions or job promotions, should focus on measurable *effort* rather than *skill*. In fact, when people speak of "meritocracy," they are often referring to this: merit means diligence, dedication, years of education, and so forth. Meritocracy is about recognizing how much effort someone has put into preparing for the exam, not just their exam performance. While measuring effort may pose challenges, it is an idea worth investigating. It might a priori achieve something closer to equality of conditions without resorting to controversial mechanisms such as race-based selection or equalizing incomes across citizens. Yet, it bumps into an important conceptual problem: those naturally more gifted might also be the ones exerting the most effort, due to inherent incentives. So, even with effort as the benchmark for merit, the outcome might still fall short of genuine equality.

To clarify this point, which is somewhat subtle, let us make a thought experiment where early childhood conditions determine 100 percent of our learning abilities. An extra hour of daily work has more effect on learning when one has more capacity to learn. In this hypothetical world, those who have been better endowed not only have better grades but also work harder. This is because each hour they spend on textbooks and assignments allows them to learn more than others would learn in that hour. So, even if the elite was selected based on effort, it would be 100 percent composed of those with good early childhood conditions. They are endowed with more ability but also work hard and thus seem more deserving. This world can be seen as meritocratic (those who are rewarded are also those who put in more effort). It is efficient (the most capable work harder and get better grades), but its fairness is highly questionable since success would purely be based on early childhood conditions. Of course, in the real world, things are messier: abilities are not 100 percent determined by early childhood but affected by multiple factors. Merit and luck come in at every stage.

Such situations, where talent makes effort more valuable, and therefore where the most deserving are also the most successful, are present everywhere: in school, the workplace, or sports. We are not surprised that someone who is not six foot three does not practice basketball all that much, and no one would claim that this is due to a lack of moral fortitude. But we fail to make the same adjustment in the workplace or at school. The economist Peter Andre calls this "shallow meritocracy." We feel morally satisfied to reward effort but fail to recognize that people who have weaker incentives—for instance, because they are less skilled, less healthy, or discriminated against—work less hard precisely because their effort is less rewarded.[7]

Rewarding Relative Effort

Economist and political scientist John Roemer concludes that reconciling meritocracy and equality of conditions requires the reward not of absolute effort but of *relative* effort within a group of homogeneous abilities.[8] The logic corresponds to boxing weight divisions: one does not put a flyweight boxer in front of a heavyweight. Taken to its extreme, this is similar to the logic of *affirmative action*, under which Harvard should, say, admit the top 1 percent of whites, Asians, Blacks, and Latinos, which would then make the racial composition of Harvard the same as that of the country.

If race were a perfect determinant of schooling ability (for instance, because it correlated perfectly with parental education or local school quality), this logic would be perfectly fair: it would introduce meritocracy within a homogeneous population. But of course that is not the case. Race is a somewhat fuzzy categorization. Also, it correlates only imperfectly with family and educational background—there are a lot of middle-class, educated Black families and poor, uneducated white families.

Economists Cappelen and Tungodden call Roemer's ethics "choice egalitarianism": it does not hold individuals responsible for any factor beyond their control. It is a form of meritocracy closer to affirmative action. It is defined in opposition to what they call "meritocratism," which holds individuals responsible for both their effort and their ability, but not for pure luck as libertarians would do. Meritocratism is closer to the pure meritocracy logic of SFFA.[9]

Overall, Roemer's proposed tweak makes meritocracy more acceptable under the veil of ignorance: if I end up in an underrepresented minority (racial, social, or other), I will get help for university admission. Thus, before knowing where I will stand, I consider the admission process as just.

Socio-determinism: What Can We Be Held Responsible For?

The force of Roemer's approach is to propose a systematic manner to reconcile meritocracy with the ideal of equality of conditions. But it remains quite theoretical: the frontier between exogenous circumstances (that we cannot be held responsible for) and preferences and choices (that we are responsible for) is in fact quite blurry, practically but also conceptually. Centuries of philosophical and religious quarrels on predestination (the religious version of determinism) versus free will have not settled the issue.

Think about the factors in life we do not control versus those we do. For instance, if I didn't read much in my youth because I became passionate about computer games, is that my fault? Or was my addiction to video games coming from factors beyond my control, such as my genetic coding, or simply a lack of parental control? Likewise, do we view young delinquents as mere products of their backgrounds? How much blame do they truly own? The complex interplay between social determinism and individual responsibility underpins the long-standing divide between left-wing and right-wing views on juvenile crime.

To address this challenge, Roemer borrows from the philosopher Ronald Dworkin the idea that we can draw a distinction between a person's *resources* and a person's *preferences* and argues along with him that "people should be held responsible for their preferences but not their resources."[10] In his approach, he embraces the determinism of economic models: once preferences and resources are known, we can compute the individual choices that automatically result. The only thing that makes effort vary once we control for resources are differences in preferences. For instance, Robert and Jameel come from middle-class families and grew up in the same neighborhood. But Robert likes to party more, while Jameel enjoys spending time with textbooks. Because Jameel works harder, he ends up with a better paid job than Robert. To Dworkin and Roemer, their career difference is just: it reflects differences in preferences (to party vs. to study), not differences in family backgrounds.

But as this example makes clear, it is somewhat bizarre to hold people responsible for their preferences, because preferences do not depend on their free will. The few models that touch on the formation of preferences actually insist on the fact that they do depend on circumstances: if I was not exposed to eating vegetables during childhood, chances are that I will not like them much as an adult. This suggests that my responsibility for poor food habits is only partial. However, if your love of music led you to become an artsy guitarist after earning your MBA, the fact that you earn less than your investment banker classmate is not unfair: it feels like you own that choice.

To handle this difficulty, Dworkin refines his definition of preferences by casting a subtle distinction between cravings that we would rather not incur (say, a very strong appetite for sugar), which he categorizes as "resources," and tastes that we really embrace and identify with (say, a passion for travel or luxury goods) and that we are thus responsible for.[11] But these classifications leave ample scope for disagreement. Roemer suggests categorizing as resources only factors that are widely perceived as beyond our control, like parental wealth or race. This approach leads to redistributive measures that should be more universally accepted.

The Era of Data-Driven Parenting

Roemer's solution doesn't address another issue of meritocracy: when only the top percentile from each category is chosen for the "winners' club," competition skyrockets to ensure children rank high in the admission process. Meritocratic pressure takes over family life.

From a utilitarian standpoint, this can be inefficient. Meritocratic pressure results in an overinvestment in attributes valued by school admissions committees. So, children are raised from the age of four to optimally pass the holistic reviews of higher education, collecting the right portfolio of extracurricular activities and summer camps to stand out. The age of the "free-range child" is over. Now comes the time of "battery-caged children." Much like any arms race, this is wasteful. However, with only a fraction of students being admitted, there's no chance for a ceasefire: if everyone is meticulously crafting their child's résumé, who would willingly step back?

A recent book intended for young parents is a perfect example of this meritocratic angst. It presents itself as a "*data-driven* guide to parenting to make better family decisions." To avoid misunderstandings, the publisher adds: "A mini-MBA course to help moms and dads implement *best* practices on a daily basis." The book, a well-researched and entertaining guide to family "management," assumes a parodic side, but is no less serious. You have been warned: amateur parenting is dead. The reproduction of elites has become an exact science. Ignore it at your children's peril.[12]

Instrumental Knowledge

Another flaw of the pure meritocratic ideal is that it leads to a purely instrumental view of learning—the idea that learning is not an end in itself but only a step for people to climb the social ladder. Meritocratic competition leads to an educational arms race that spoils childhoods and accentuates social barriers and the homogeneity of elites. These utilitarian investments divert minds from the tortuous paths of intellectual discovery and the ideal of nondirected curiosity. To earn points in the meritocracy game, it is more effective to push one's children to take Python or statistics courses than to read Dostoyevsky or Steinbeck. Hyper-meritocracy leads to the evaluation of humans on the one-dimensional scale of social success. It does not encourage self-discovery, originality, or the construction of one's own identity. In a recent interview, Kwame Anthony Appiah, who has taught philosophy in several major US universities, expressed his disappointment that such a large fraction of the elite that he helped to train went into investment banking or consulting. He sees this as a failure of the American educational system.[13]

Meritocratic Hubris

Philosophers have discussed other drawbacks of pure meritocracy. Michael Sandel notes that meritocracy legitimizes inequalities between winners and losers in society.[14] Unlike the old social order, in which aristocrats only owed their positions to the luck of being born into the right family, the meritocratic order crowns members of the elite as superior beings, simply because they are the most deserving ones. Having won the competition for top jobs, they do not consider themselves indebted to the rest of society. Sandel calls this attitude "meritocratic hubris." Meritocratic elites secede and conflate justice with social Darwinism. Nonachievers must "know their place," know how to not be sore losers, concede defeat with fair play, as in sports tournaments. Consistent with this idea, several social psychology experiments do indicate that individuals who believe in meritocracy accept inequalities more easily, even if they are not on the side of the winners.[15]

Sandel's idea is not new. An earlier account can be found in Michael Young's *Rise of Meritocracy*, published in 1958. In this exercise in sociology fiction, Young imagines that, in the future, British society has become a perfect meritocracy. In this futuristic society, children are selected based on their aptitudes, which are evaluated by a benevolent and sophisticated educational system. Regardless of their background, skin color, or gender, gifted children receive the best education and join the country's ruling elite. Others go directly to the lower classes of society where they are treated with humanity, but as inferiors. The lower classes are mostly docile to the social order. They consider themselves lucky to benefit from a protective state and the enlightened stewardship of the elite.

Young's thought experiment makes a simple point: a society can be perfectly meritocratic without being just. It can be a dystopian nightmare that locks people into rigid social classes, without hope or perspective. Ironically, the word *meritocracy*, a neologism coined by the author to describe this sociological nightmare, was immediately adopted by commentators with a positive connotation. Young's dystopia has become the official utopia of our modern societies.

To conclude this discussion, meritocracy is of course a valuable social objective (we must fight for equal rights and against inequality of opportunity), but it cannot, on its own, define what a "good society" is. The "pure" meritocratic ideal is morally dubious. There is the obvious truism that success is always due in part to luck. But, more subtly, a meritocratic society is at risk of drifting toward a modern form of aristocracy, where merit legitimizes social hierarchies of wealth and power and the secession of elites. Finally, a world in which the accumulation of good grades would be the sole objective of individuals would be a sociological inferno, a modern version of the Hobbesian war of all against all.

We have spent most of this chapter discussing fairness pluralism in the context of university admissions. We chose this example because it is important and pedagogically helpful. But there are many other situations in which people's views of fairness are diverse and sophisticated. We propose to end this discussion with a short presentation of two other examples of fairness pluralism: taxes and algorithms.

Taxation: What Is Really Optimal?

When economists think about taxes, they have a very specific approach in mind: They seek to minimize "distortions," that is, the loss of GDP coming from taxing people. For instance, taxing people's salaries discourages them from working. So, too much income tax reduces GDP. Taxing capital hurts savings and investment even more. So, to raise a given amount of money for public services, it is more efficient to tax labor income than capital income. This type of reasoning is called "optimal taxation": we tax relatively less where it hurts the most (and relatively more where it hurts the least).

"Optimal taxation" is not at all how people think about taxes. A prominent example is estate taxation. Taxing inherited wealth is perceived as being relatively efficient since there is no evidence that estate tax discourages parents from working hard to pass on their wealth to their offspring. So, it is an easy way for the government to collect money, without hurting entrepreneurial dynamism, innovation, and growth. It is more efficient than, say, taxing people's salaries—which has been proven to curb incentives to work and therefore hurt the economy. The rest of the population, however, strongly disagrees. The economist Stefanie Stantcheva has done extensive work on people's perceptions of the economy, especially about taxes. In the United States, only about one-third of those surveyed support raising estate taxes (about 40 percent of Democrats and less than 20 percent of Republicans).[16] In France, only 21 percent think it is fair to tax the inheritance of wealthy parents who have worked all their lives (for the case of parents who have not worked, the percentage rises to 31 percent).[17] Why is this the case? One option is to assume (as economists are sometimes inclined to do) that people do not understand what is good for them. A less paternalistic alternative is that they have, in these matters, libertarian ethics: they see inheritance taxes as unfair because property, deserved or not, is somehow sacred—it is not to be violated unless it arose from extortion.

Another example of the rejection of the "optimal taxation" principle is the carbon tax debate. According to economic logic, taxing carbon is optimal, in the sense that it discourages greenhouse gas emissions while letting those who are most in need to burn fossil fuels (they will find it worthwhile to pay the tax). It is almost unanimously supported by economists but widely rejected in the polls. When asked about the alternative between a carbon tax and environmental standards for car manufacturers, 22 percent of US respondents supported the carbon tax, compared to 92 percent of economists.[18] As in the estate tax debate, some have invoked the "confused citizen hypothesis": people do not realize how optimal such a tax would be. It seems, however, that people are *not* more likely to accept this policy if they are more informed about it.[19] Confusion thus does not seem to explain the rejection of the carbon tax (or at least cannot be the entire story).

As for estate taxation, it is not difficult to figure out fairness-related reasons that would lead individuals to reject the carbon tax. An obvious one is the unequal effects of such a tax. Since its objective is to modify behavior (encourage people to take public transportation or consume less gasoline), the ones who will pay the tax are precisely those who have no other choice: people who cannot bike to work or who do not have access to public transportation. In addition, this tax can be perceived as a moral indictment, a sin tax imposed by righteous big-city elites who can afford to walk to the office. Taxes are not just a way to change behavior, as economists tend to think. They are often perceived as a way for society to indicate which behavior is right and which one is wrong. Of course, economics research has looked for ways to undo this perception by setting up a transfer to low-income people who cannot reduce carbon emissions. Such technocratic fixes may increase the perceived fairness of the policy, but they typically run against issues of trust in government.[20]

Such hostility to optimal taxation can be found in many settings, such as the "city congestion charge" popular among public finance economists. To reduce traffic, some big cities (London, New York) impose a tax on whoever drives a car into the city center. Inspired by this debate, we asked German, French, and American participants in our survey whether they would support such a scheme:

> Faced with numerous traffic jams in his/her city, a mayor is considering
>
> - imposing a $15 toll at the entrance to the city, that allows drivers to drive around the city for one day. Those who do not pay must use other modes of transportation [half of the sample]
> - reducing the number of parking spaces and increasing pedestrian streets to discourage drivers who do not absolutely need to take their car into the city [half of the sample]
>
> What do you think about this initiative? Rate from 1 to 10, where 1 means it is better to do nothing and 10 means it is a good solution.

This question deals with urban congestion and two alternative policy responses: (1) imposing a congestion tax, or (2) removing parking spots and making car drivers' lives miserable. Economic research strongly favors the first option, because it follows the principles of optimal taxation. Exactly like the carbon tax, it will reduce traffic from those who can find alternatives. Other drivers will pay the toll, but they will benefit from a less congested city. The second option (making car drivers' lives miserable) is less efficient but has the advantage of leveling the playing field: everyone, rich or poor, will suffer the same.

Respondents strongly reject the congestion charge. The average level of support for the parking space reduction policy is between 5.5 in the United States and 5.9 in France. It is not high (unsurprisingly) but still much higher than support for the congestion charge, which is 4.3 in the United States and 4.1 in France. The rejection of optimal taxation is thus strong in the population. The magnitude of this rejection does not differ by partisan affiliation, so there might be a mixture of motivations. It may be perceived on the left as an unfair tax on the poor, and on the right as an unacceptable limitation of the freedom of movement. Another hypothesis is that, in the second option, avoidance strategies are not more accessible to wealthier people: it will take more time to park, but everyone will face the same constraint, rich or poor. The second option is thus considered fairer by everyone. Our data unfortunately do not shed light on this, but this is an interesting topic for further research.

Fairness and Algorithms

Before concluding this chapter, let us discuss one last instance in which people's view of fairness is somewhat sophisticated and surprising: the ethics of artificial intelligence. This issue gives rise to a lively literature on the borders of several disciplines: moral psychology, law, ethics, economics, and computer science. Nowadays, there are algorithms for judicial decision-making (bail decisions), medical diagnosis (identifying cancers), human resource management (identifying candidates to interview from a large number of potential recruits), bank lending decisions, and so on. In these situations, the same questions arise as in the Harvard trial.[21] Should those with a history of crime or those who live on the South Side of Chicago be denied bail more often? Given that they are, on average, more likely to be Black, isn't this akin to racial discrimination? To be fair, should the algorithm be purely based on the predictor variables (history of crime, address), or should it mitigate the effect of skin color?

Another problem is that algorithms are calibrated on previous human decisions, which also creates biases. Imagine, for example, that a large firm wants to hire people who are less likely to quit because it needs to train them before they can become productive. The HR department sets up an algorithm that prescreens applications to concentrate interviewer time on the most promising candidates. The algorithm is calibrated on the data of past applications and hiring decisions that the firm has collected. Now, assume that, in the past, the firm was mostly interviewing men. Past data will thus be very useful to predict which male applicants are the most promising. However, the algorithm will be much less insightful when it comes to female applicants. As a result, the firm will end up mostly interviewing and hiring men. A vicious circle then kicks in: as the company continues to use the algorithm, the dataset expands, but it contains more and more men. This is the classic trade-off between exploration and exploitation: predictive algorithms exploit existing information but do not explore enough to reverse injustice.[22]

What criterion of justice should be imposed on algorithms? According to surveys, and as in the college admissions case, participants' views of what is fair are not obvious. Take the case of an algorithm that detects serious diseases. Here, a majority of people favor maximum accuracy (the best that technology allows), even if this accuracy is unevenly distributed (for instance, an algorithm detecting lung cancer in X-rays that works better for women than men seems acceptable). In contrast, for the detection of benign diseases, people strongly believe that the algorithm should aim for the same level of accuracy on all sociodemographic sub-groups, even if it means limiting technological accuracy for some.[23] Thus, they opt for strict equality in diagnosing benign diseases but for efficiency in life-and-death situations. One exciting area for future research is to understand when people switch from one view of fairness to another (a bit like, in chapter 2, how we saw that people oscillate between rule-based and consequence-based altruism).

Fairness and Pluralism

Multiple laboratory experiments in the economics literature have shown that individuals strongly care about fairness. People reject sharing rules that they consider unfair, even if doing so is costly to them. People reward generous sharing decisions by working harder, in an attempt to reciprocate. However, the literature finds that the criteria for defining fairness vary according to the context and the people involved. On a case-by-case basis, people have relatively strong views on what is fair. We have described, in this chapter, how complex people's perceptions of fairness are. They are not absurd, though: complexity arises because equally coherent views of fairness can contradict one another.

Faced with such unpredictability, we believe no single group of people (technocrats, reporters, academics, politicians) has the legitimacy to impose their own view of what is fair or unfair. In democracies, the view that voters hold needs to be part of the conversation. Running surveys that expose individuals to the classic moral dilemmas of public policy is an important first step to incorporate people's moral preferences into economic policymaking.

6

Local and Global

In public debates, economists most often play advocates of globalization. They defend economic reforms that lift obstacles to economic exchanges. They are typically favorable to encouraging legal immigration. They often consider that global governance, through supranational institutions such as the World Trade Organization or the European Union, is necessary.

This proglobalization sentiment does not stand in a vacuum but is based on solid conceptual arguments: comparative advantages, interdependence of nations, circulation of talent (essential in the knowledge economy), and multilateralism (crucial at a time of financial and climate crises). The gain from trade between two countries is for an economics professor one of the most pleasant lectures to give. Conceptually, it produces a real "aha moment," an eye-opening effect. Students understand something they had not grasped before. The notion of comparative advantage, which determines activities countries should specialize in, is deep, yet surprising and somewhat counterintuitive. The fact that two countries are better off trading with each other than not trading—because of specialization in comparative advantages—is also nonobvious. Even more thought-provoking is the result that, even if your trade partner is protectionist (taxes your exports), the most efficient decision you can make is to not be protectionist yourself (that is, not tax your imports). Turning the other cheek pays off.

The general population does not buy it, however. Take the question: "On average, have Americans benefited from free trade with Mexico and Canada?" In a survey of academic economic experts, 95 percent answered yes to the question, compared to only 46 percent of a representative sample of the American population.[1] Or ask survey participants to evaluate the following statement: "Trade with China improves living conditions for most Americans because goods imported from China are cheaper." Again, while 95 percent of economic experts agree, only 20 percent of Americans do.[2] Moreover, it seems that the public cares little about the advice of economists. When respondents are told about the economic consensus on trade, their opinion is barely changed.

We have sympathy for globalization enthusiasts. In our own country, we have written our fair share of opinion pieces underlining the benefits of trade with China and the cost of protectionism. But we have always had reservations about the unbridled enthusiasm for free trade and the allergy to protectionism that is common in the profession. Of course, going full-on autarkic is not a desirable outcome. The logic of comparative advantages is sound and makes us richer. But it does not strike us as obvious that "zero protectionism" is the only rational approach. Given the noneconomic costs of globalization, some middle ground needs to be found. This chapter is about these noneconomic costs.

The Academic Consensus

Let us start with the current state of the academic consensus on free trade. Without training in economics, one tends to see international trade as a zero-sum game: jobs created in the South are destroyed in the North. This view is implicit in the term "offshoring": nothing changes, and jobs are just transferred offshore, moving from here to there. However, an important contribution of economic models is to show that the zero-sum perspective is misleading and that trade can be a win-win proposition. It allows each party to specialize in what it does best, relative to the others, to maximize the total value generated. For example, assume Fatou and Kevin live together in a house. They both enjoy eating good food and taking in the view of a beautiful backyard. Now, assume Fatou is both a better gardener and a better cook than Kevin, and that Kevin really is a terrible gardener. Plants die when he touches them. The theory of comparative advantage then tells us that Fatou should concentrate on gardening, and Kevin on cooking (instead of each one doing a little of both activities).

This theory of comparative advantage was, in the eyes of the economist Paul Samuelson, one of very few economic theories that was both true and nontrivial.[3] This may explain why economists and the general public disagree. The public might need to be educated to fully grasp the benefits of free trade. Some economists have spent considerable energy trying to explain the logic of comparative advantages and the pitfall of protectionism. For example, Nobel laureate Paul Krugman began his career as a public intellectual by defending the benefits of international trade against the nonacademic economists who defended protectionism (at that time against Japan).[4]

The Losers of Globalization

Another explanation of why economists and noneconomists disagree on globalization is that, while free trade is an overall net positive for the economy, it does hurt part of the population: those whose jobs are destroyed by international competition. To be sure, the "losers" of globalization were never forgotten by economic theory; the unequal effects of globalization has been at the heart of models since at least the 1940s. As income inequality exploded in the United States during the 1980s and 1990s, economists were quick to point to imports as a potential suspect. The consensus of the profession, however, quickly converged to the idea that the effect of globalization on inequality was negligible. In a nutshell, the "job content of imports" (the number of jobs that would be created by relocating factories in the home country) was too small to explain the rise in inequality in the United States or mass unemployment in Europe. Put differently, if we decided to repatriate the production of T-shirts to the United States instead of importing them from emerging economies, we would have factories mostly populated by machines, not by workers. We would not create many jobs.

By the mid-1990s, the scientific debate was considered resolved. The stagnation of low incomes in the United States came from the replacement of workers by machines, and the destruction of jobs due to globalization was too small to worry about. In policy circles, the consensus was that free trade was a good thing and that political push-back came from implementation errors. What was needed was more pedagogy (the public opinion was misinformed) and some redistribution (to subsidize the losers). In mainstream economics, Dani Rodrik was a rare voice arguing for a more critical appraisal of globalization, which in his view needed saving from its "cheerleaders." To Rodrik, the antiglobalization sentiment needed to be taken seriously, rather than being dismissed by the elites as an exaggeration. By the mid-2000s, international trade was already "free enough"; there was no need to further irritate public opinion by signing more trade agreements.[5] He also advocated a healthy dose of protectionism and the rehabilitation of industrial policy.

In the early 2010s, the link between trade and jobs was revisited by a new generation of economists, who focused on China's entry into the World Trade Organization. The shocking result was that this "China shock" had indeed contributed to one-quarter of the drop in US manufacturing employment.[6] Yet the proglobalization sentiment among economists barely moved. At the end of an article entitled "Globalization: What Did We Miss?," which takes stock of all these changes, Krugman reaffirms his belief in the virtues of free trade and his skepticism about protectionism.[7] There are losers, sure enough, but it should be easy to find a solution based on redistribution and training, given the aggregate gains. The new consensus could be summarized as follows: "Free trade has increased the size of the pie; politicians have not done a good job at sharing the gains between people equitably. Please take your complaints to the political science department."

Compensating the Losers of Globalization Is More Difficult Than It Seems

An important assumption that underlies proglobalization sentiment is that one can separate economic and social choices. To evaluate a reform, economists determine if it is good on aggregate (summing up all the effects within the country). If the reform is good on aggregate, they argue politicians should then fine-tune redistribution (via targeted subsidies and taxes) to target a socially acceptable sharing of the aggregate gains of trade.

A major obstacle to this "separation theorem" (growing the pie vs. sharing the pie) is that taking from the winners to give to the losers is far from easy. The first roadblock is defining who benefits and who suffers from globalization. Workers who lose their jobs because of production offshoring are clear-cut cases of "losers." But what about the factory accountant, who can easily find a similar job at a different firm? Further, isn't the hairdresser whose salon is next to the factory also a victim of globalization? What about the town's inhabitants, whose parks will no longer be maintained by the company's local taxes and whose houses lose value? The effects of offshoring on the local economy are complex and indirectly affect a lot of people. Who is hurt, and to what extent, is hard to measure.

An additional complication is that taxes and subsidies change people's behavior. This makes some transfers unfeasible—a fact known to all economists. The winners of globalization are holders of human and financial capital. They are mobile and sensitive to taxation. Taxing capital, like taxing people's incomes, has a cost: it reduces production by discouraging work and investment. Symmetrically, subsidizing those who suffer from offshoring could reduce their willingness to retrain and to change places and careers. Thus, sharing the spoils of globalization more equally across different economic agents is not feasible without deadweight loss. It is not a matter of just "splitting the pie." In fact, it could very well be that deadweight losses exceed the gains of globalization.

Noneconomic Cost

Besides, globalization has noneconomic effects that cannot simply be redistributed. On this point, applied economic analysis is particularly blind. One cannot just compensate people for losing their jobs with a government check. A job is not just a way to make money. It also provides meaning, human relationships, self-esteem, social status, and a sense that one contributes to society.

These nonpecuniary aspects are not included in economic cost-benefit analyses run by policymakers. Yet, they are important, possibly larger than the gains from globalization. In the latest release of the European Values Study (realized between 2017 and 2021 in thirty-six countries), more than 52 percent of the respondents agree that "it is humiliating receiving money without working," and 71 percent agree that "to fully develop your talents, you need to have a job."[8] Economists Andrew Clark and Andrew Oswald find that losing their jobs makes people about two times more unhappy than going through a divorce or the death of a relative.[9] An experiment conducted in refugee camps confirms the importance of this emotional dimension of jobs. In this experiment, some participants got paid to do nothing. They reported the same level of well-being as the control group (which received neither money nor work). Some participants were paid (as much) in exchange for doing some work. They reported being happier. The emotional comfort coming from work cannot be substituted by cash transfers equivalent to a wage.[10] Overall, work is not just about getting paid; it brings fulfillment, dignity, purpose.

Another important nonmonetary cost that cost-benefit analysis typically ignores is mobility: sometimes finding a job requires moving. But people cannot be transplanted from one place to the next like potatoes that can be replanted in a new location. Here again, the psychological cost of moving to a new city, which involves leaving behind friends and family, is assumed to be negligible in baseline economic analysis, which focuses on monetary incomes.

Last, workers are right to fear the alignment of social standards to the lowest denominator. Free trade forces companies to be competitive with the rest of the world. Pressure to lower social standards emerges, especially when it is the only way to keep local companies alive. The competition from foreign companies that are not subject to similar constraints can be perceived as unfair, and workers ask for protection against it.

Together, these objections may explain why protectionist measures, absurd to most economists, can appeal to public opinion. For example, Paola Sapienza and Luigi Zingales find that 75 percent of Americans believe that a "Buy American Act" can create jobs (compared to 11 percent of economists).[11] In a similar vein, a survey by Rafael Di Tella and Dani Rodrik describes to American participants the hypothetical situation of a manufacturing plant that closes for various reasons (management error, obsolete products, international competition).[12] When the facility is shut down because of international competition, especially competition from low-wage countries, survey participants favor protectionist measures over cash compensation. They prefer to block imports and keep the company alive, rather than letting free trade and public transfers turn the workers' lives upside down. Perhaps they suspect that such transfers are impossible or will not be enough to offset the damage.

Distorting Competition to Preserve Local Employment

To summarize: international trade has benefits, but it also has noneconomic costs (it is difficult to redistribute its gains, there are potentially large noneconomic costs). That said, it could very well be that people see the costs, but ignore the benefits of trade. Consistent with this, Stefanie Stantcheva and her coauthors have documented the prevalence of "zero-sum" thinking in US public opinion, the idea that economic transactions do not create value, that one's own gains are exactly balanced by someone else's losses.[13] Roughly one-third of their survey respondents hold this view of the economy on a variety of issues. These respondents are likely to view trade as a zero net gain for the United States and protectionism as a costless way of avoiding moving resources from the working class to the rich. "We can save our jobs, without hurting the economy."

Now, if people knew that protectionism was costly, would they still support it? To answer this, we have in our international survey a question that constrains respondents to take the economic costs of protectionism into account. It is formulated as follows:

> In order to support a local manufacturer, the authorities have imposed on your city's transport company to buy only streetcars manufactured by a [two assumptions: national/European] company. However, this would increase the fare by [three assumptions: 5%, 10%, or 50%], but it will save 1,000 jobs in the region.
>
> How much do you agree with this initiative? Rate from 1 to 10: where 1 means you strongly disagree and 10 means you strongly agree.

We vary, across participants (and randomly), the price to pay to protect the local manufacturer. The cost of transportation paid locally would increase by 5 percent, 10 percent, or 50 percent to preserve local jobs. We also vary the proximity to the "local" manufacturer. Half of the participants are told the local manufacturer is "national" (in the United States we use the term "local," which could correspond to a region or even a state). The other half are told the firm is "European" (in the United States we use the phrase "from the USA").

What do we observe? First, the French, Germans, and Americans strongly support the logic of saving jobs, even if it means a significant additional cost. Even with a 50 percent increase in ticket prices, the average approval level is 6.1 in France and the United States (and 5.5 in Germany), well into the "approval" territory. These results show strong anxiety about deindustrialization in all three countries. Second, people are sensitive to the cost. If the intervention only leads to a 5 percent increase in ticket prices, the average support is between 7.1 and 7.4. Third, in France and Germany, approval does not depend on whether the firm is national or European. Similarly, American respondents support evenly local or national firms. This suggests a level of European solidarity that could be similar to the solidarity across US states.

Finally, support for the protectionist intervention does not depend on political leanings but reflects "collectivist" values. This finding echoes our earlier discussion on competition (chapter 4). As in chapter 4, we measure "collectivism" as the average strength of agreement with values of fairness, compassion, loyalty to the in-group, and authority. Participants who strongly value all four dimensions are those who care less about the individual and more about the community. They are found in equal numbers among conservatives and progressives. We find the most collectivist half of our respondents approve of the protectionist measure at 6.7, versus 6.1 for the most individualistic half. Overall, protectionism is popular but more so among people who aspire to a strong community to the detriment of the individual (the "Durkheimian half" of the population, as we argued in chapter 4). These aspirations are found in equal amounts among progressives and conservatives, a point already discussed in chapter 4 and famously highlighted by moral psychologist Jonathan Haidt.[14]

Moral Sovereignty: Upholding Social and Environmental Standards

Another factor that can motivate banning some imports is when they come from countries where social or environmental standards are low and are incompatible with what we think should be the norm. Importing goods from countries with lower social standards is not only seen as a threat to our own norms and jobs at home. Consumers might see it as being complacent with bad things happening abroad, as being complicit with immoral acts. There is a long history of consumer boycotts, from Nike in the 1990s (whose suppliers employed children) to Foxconn,

Apple's supplier, in the 2010s (whose brutal working conditions led to a slew of employee suicides). In chapter 8, we will discuss in more detail studies showing that consumers are morally motivated, but let us focus here on international trade.

A particularly salient example of morally motivated import bans is the weaponization of trade with Russia after the 2022 invasion of Ukraine. European countries were motivated by compassion for Ukrainians, whom they considered victims of an unjust and particularly cruel military attack. But they also felt that Europe needed to defend itself against an increasingly bellicose neighbor: banning oil and gas imports from Russia could potentially weaken the economy and the regime. This was not the first time the international community decided to sanction a country that was perceived as threatening by trying to cut it off from global trade routes: we recall South Africa in the 1980s, Iran in the 2000s, and so on. That such sanctions are effective is, to say the very least, debated, but that discussion would be too much of a detour for this book.[15]

The willingness of European citizens to sacrifice their well-being to sanction Russia was real, but limited. "We need to accept to pay the price of our freedom and of our values," said French president Emmanuel Macron in August 2022.[16] But what price? A survey conducted among the German population showed that there was widespread agreement with the principles of economic sanctions on Russia. Sixty-seven percent of the respondents said they would accept a fuel price rise if this would increase pressure on Russia. While support was broad-based, however, the willingness to pay for it was quite limited. The share of respondents willing to accept a rise of more than 25 percent in fuel prices was less than 20 percent. Thus, Germans were willing to make an effort but not one that would significantly constrain their economy or Russia.[17]

Another example of the link between trade and morality is climate change. European companies have long been advocating for carbon tariffs that would correct the gap in environmental norms between Europe and its trading partners. Europe imposes high carbon taxes on its home production. These carbon taxes are higher than those in other countries, so, inevitably, productive activities that are carbon-intensive (steelworks, car manufacturing, and so on) will slip away from Europe. This not only is damaging for European manufacturing but also makes efforts to decarbonize quite vain. One ton of CO_2 has the same impact on climate, whether it is produced in Europe or elsewhere. This justifies establishing carbon-based tariffs to tax imported goods.

CO_2 emissions are easy to measure, but the debate on social standards is less clear-cut. Regarding child labor, for instance, economists point to the fact that boycotting may harm, rather than benefit, child workers. Families in poor countries that were making a living from exports might fall further down into poverty. They sometimes just do not have the option to let their children go to school. It is not just cold, calculating economists who make the case for child labor. The philosopher Will MacAskill, one of the leading figures of the effective altruism movement (see chapter 2), argues that such boycotting is morally wrong since in many cases child labor does promote school attendance.[18] Still, boycotting could provide incentives to suppliers and lawmakers in developing countries to improve their social standards.

To evaluate people's willingness to ban imports for moral reasons, we have written a question designed to help understand the different moral motivations behind protectionism. In the question, protectionism is economically costly (it increases import prices by 10 percent) but is accompanied by various moral benefits (randomized across participants). The question is formulated as follows:

> The government is proposing a new tax on clothing imported from countries [one of three options]:
>
> - that have weaker environmental standards than [participant country] (one-third of the sample);
> - that have weaker social standards than [participant country] (one-third of the sample);
> - that do not respect human rights (one-third of the sample).

> Because of the tax, your clothing would increase by approximately 10%. How much do you agree with this initiative? Rate from 1 to 10, where 1 means you strongly disagree and 10 means you strongly agree.

As we saw in the previous question, support for the protectionist policy is on average strong, with an average rating of 6.1 across moral causes and countries. French respondents display stronger support (6.6), and US participants the weakest (still 5.8). Human rights seem the most legitimate reason to bear costly import taxes (average rating 6.6), social standards being the least acceptable (still 5.8). As before, again, we also find that individuals who adhere more strongly to collective values are more likely to accept the protectionist measure. The rating difference between the most collectivist and the most individualistic half is large, 0.9 in France and 0.4 in the United States. Again, the Durkheimian logic of the previous question is at work. Individualists are more likely to see the realms of morality and the market as separate.

Identity, Culture, and Protectionism

Globalization also collides with national identities, especially when imported goods and services have a strong cultural dimension. This is another example of a nonmonetary effect that we believe tends to be neglected in applied economic analysis.

It may not matter much where our televisions or cars come from, but the same cannot be said for our meals, movies, or even landscapes (which we monetize through tourism). Food is a particularly salient case of cultural good. For instance, David Atkin, Eve Colson-Sihra, and Moses Shayo provide evidence that, during interethnic conflicts in India, Muslims are more likely to eat beef (forbidden to Hindus) and Hindus are less likely to eat meat (as a way to distinguish themselves from Muslims).[19] Popular support for the logic of agricultural protectionism in Europe and Japan is one of the reasons for the failure of the Doha negotiations, the latest round of multilateral (WTO-backed) world trade agreements.[20]

Beyond food, all cultural industries (think: media, cinema, TV, books, video games) are closely linked to our identities. Economists Daniel Cohen and Thierry Verdier describe cultural industries as characterized by high fixed but low variable costs.[21] For instance, shooting a movie is expensive (it's a big, one-off cost), but showing it in theaters or on TV costs almost nothing. With this type of structure, the size of the domestic market provides a competitive advantage that is hard to beat. Cultural goods amortized on large populations can be sold at low cost throughout the world. Another advantage of large economies is that they are often culturally diverse (the United States, India, Brazil, the "Anglo-Saxon" world, for example). Such diversity encourages cultural firms to develop products that are acceptable to all, thus facilitating global distribution. In this context, small cultures risk being overwhelmed by cultural goods from large countries, appealing to broad audiences and sold at predatory prices.

Smaller nations try to resist, of course. This push toward cultural preservation is not just about nostalgia. It is about keeping their unique story alive in today's global world. The concern is that if they do not actively promote their traditions and language, future generations will drift away from their roots. Educated with cheaper global cultural products, tastes will tilt toward the dominant influence of larger nations, and smaller cultures will disappear. "Cultural biodiversity" will suffer.

The solution often chosen is, as in the case of agriculture, protectionism. To preserve their own cultural sector and identity, smaller economies have no choice but to tax or limit imports of cultural goods and subsidize domestic creation. This is the logic of the "cultural exception," a logic to which our own country, France, is particularly attached, to the point of having made it a deal-breaker during the 2014 Europe–US trade negotiations. For example, French law[22] requires radio stations, whether public or private, to broadcast 40 percent of songs in French, a regulation inspired by Québec. In the same spirit, the preservation of local languages, such as Catalan in Spain or Gaelic in Ireland, is based on active public interventions preventing the general use of the dominant language (Spanish and English) and imposing the use of the local dialect in official communications.

Immigration: Economics and Beyond

It is impossible to conclude our discussion of the noneconomic effects of globalization without mentioning the debate on immigration. The economic consensus on immigration is overwhelmingly positive. A famous empirical study by David Card, a Nobel laureate in economics, is often mentioned.[23] In this study, Card looks at the effects of the mass influx of Cuban immigrants to Miami in 1982 (the backdrop for Brian De Palma's movie *Scarface*). He finds that this shock did not hurt the working conditions of locals. The consensus of the literature is that absorbing first-generation immigrants is not that hard.[24] A contributing factor is that immigrants are not just employees but also entrepreneurs. It is, in a sense, the story of the protagonist of *Scarface*, a Cuban refugee who becomes a major cocaine trafficker: he does not take a job from an American drug dealer. Another argument is that descendants of immigrants tend to do better than natives, and natives sometimes even *benefit* from the arrival of immigrants locally, as economics is not a zero-sum game.[25]

There is also a large body of literature pointing to the key role of immigrants in US universities and the innovation ecosystem, and their overrepresentation among talented engineers, start-up founders, and now even big tech CEOs. Study after study confirms that newcomers file more patents and write more research papers than natives.[26] This idyllic picture often fails to mention the perverse effects of this *brain drain*, which is good for the "drainer," but not so nice for the "drainee." Entrepreneurs and inventors who work in the United States do not work in their home country, which is thus not benefiting from their talent.

If immigration is so beneficial, then, why does the general population of developed countries express such an aversion to it? For some, people simply overestimate the problem. When asked about the share of immigrants in their own countries, survey participants tend to overestimate it by a large margin.[27] A series of polls have shown that Europeans and Americans surveyed overestimate the share of immigrants in the population by a factor of about two (30 percent versus less than 15 percent in reality).[28] A limitation of some of these surveys is that, while they ask about the share of foreign-born immigrants, survey respondents may also include their descendants (who are now citizens).

A related theory is that the economic benefits of immigration are like climate change. People ignore, or deny, the scientific evidence that immigrants are good for the economy. This is why economists advertise their results with so much vigor: they are hoping to make the population realize that immigration is not that big a deal (quantitatively) and that it is overall a net positive for the economy. From an economic perspective, there should be, if anything, more, not less immigration.

But the general population does not seem to care all that much about the economics of immigration. For example, it came as a surprise to social scientists that people's attitudes on the topic are not shaped at all by their personal economic interests.[29] True, more educated individuals are more favorable to immigration, but they favor low-skilled and high-skilled immigration equally; if their beliefs were motivated by self-interest, they would be against competing with skilled immigrants. All the same, less educated citizens tend to oppose immigration from the unskilled (who may compete with them), but also from the more educated individuals (who are not directly competing with them and who may even create jobs for them).

Another interesting data point is that survey participants do not fear that immigrants will take their job, as if they already knew about the Card study and the follow-up research. This is obvious, for instance, from the 2017 wave of the European Values Study (thus in the middle of the refugee crisis in Europe).[30] To the question "on a scale of 0 (agree) to 10 (disagree), immigrants take the jobs of [French/Germans/etc.]," the average response in the five largest European countries is 5.2 for

Italy, 5.7 for Spain, 6.1 for France, 6.2 for the United Kingdom, and 7.2 for Germany. So even in high-unemployment EU countries (France, Italy, and Spain), the dominant view is that immigrants do not take the jobs of locals. We have posed a similar question to our own survey participants from France, the United States, and Germany and found similar results.[31] When asked about their approval of immigration restrictions, only 5 percent (Germany) to 12 percent (United States) of participants state "Immigrants take our jobs" as the main motivation. Overall, Europeans seem to think that if immigration creates problems, it is not on the labor market.

When praising the economic virtues of immigration, economists are thus off-topic. People are not afraid of losing their jobs to migrants. They probably have no issue with welcoming the likes of Marie Curie, Steve Jobs, or Elon Musk, who will make their country rich. To them, immigration is not about economics, but comes down to tensions between moral values, whether our duty is to our national community (our culture, our language, our heritage) or to all of humanity (war refugees, economic migrants, and so on). For instance, 90 percent of Americans agree that one must speak English to be American.[32] Ninety-three percent of Europeans believe that immigrants need to speak the local language, and 89 percent think that they need to share the culture of the country they come to. There is more diversity in attitudes to assimilationism. The fraction of respondents who do *not* want immigrants to "maintain distinct customs and traditions" is around 60 percent in Scandinavian countries, the Netherlands, and Mediterranean countries, and 50 percent in France, the United Kingdom, and Germany.[33] Overall, cultural and moral issues are much more prevalent in people's attitudes to immigration than economics.

In all honesty, in this debate, economists' positions are not purely driven by economics either. They have their own moral values. Most of us economists have universalist values and are committed to diversity and meritocracy. The profession itself is a highly internationalized ecosystem, which emphasizes individual achievement (publications).

University economics departments (like those in most sciences) typically include members from all continents. We feel like blessed children of globalization and would want to convince the public that immigration is a good thing.

However, is it legitimate to let our own moral compass dictate what the larger population is allowed to aspire to? It would be unscientific to disqualify anti-immigration sentiment as "populist," if not "xenophobic," because it hurts our universalist values. As social scientists, who are neither politicians nor philosophers, we feel the most scientific course of action on that matter is to better understand how people think, rather than to dismiss their opinions as bigoted or uninformed. The utilitarianism of economists is not the only acceptable moral system when it comes to immigration. For instance, many think of the nation as a community, different in nature from an airport (where everyone is a passerby) or a supermarket (where everything is available for consumption after an economic transaction). All citizens of a nation cooperate to nurture and grow their community, its culture, its language, its cohesion. As a result, citizenship comes with rights, but also duties to other members of the community. The poorest in a given nation hold priority moral claims over their more successful compatriots. This view is shared, for instance, by the Danish social democrats, who limit immigration to preserve a strong welfare state.

For similar reasons, the preservation of identity is a perfectly acceptable reason to restrict immigration. Some social scientists dismiss these reasons as reactionary, a "cultural backlash" of old white men against the irresistible march of Western societies toward multicultural liberalism.[34] But this is a coarse, if not patronizing, view of people's practical ethics. Some may think that their national culture is not a set of consumption goods designed to make citizens feel better but a heritage that comes with (inherited or acquired) citizenship. Members of the national community have a duty to enrich and transmit it to future generations. Such a view, prevalent in our own country, requires cultural assimilation of new entrants and therefore might impose a limit on how many immigrants the country can accept.

Conclusion: "Smart Protectionism," an Oxymoron?

The economic consensus is that more free trade is good. "Smart protectionism" is perceived by economic experts as an oxymoron of bad taste: free trade is necessarily a good idea, because it maximizes the possibilities of transactions between consenting nations. But this view ignores the fact that individuals do not only care about material consumption. Globalization is a package: it helps people consume cheaper products from faraway places, but it also comes with extra economic considerations. Some people fear the threat to their identities. Others see the destruction of their industrial heartland. Overall, economies gain materially from being largely open, but these gains (which are actually not that huge)[35] are hard to redistribute fairly between winners and losers, leaving some communities scarred.

Some of us economists are uncomfortable with this pushback. A temptation is to attribute it to ignorance or prejudice. The message of this book is that we need to more systematically probe the moral preferences of people, rather than try to impose our own. It is not a priori ridiculous to refuse to import oil produced in a repressive theocracy; nor is it a priori absurd to resist the cultural grip of a country that can afford to distribute its movies at low cost and change the identity of its audiences. But, of course, as legitimate as these preferences may be, there is an economic cost to forgoing the gains of commercial exchange. It is the economists' job to inform the population about this cost, but, as we argue in this book, we also need to understand and expose the noneconomic implications of globalization.

7
Beauty

> In the presence of nature, a wild delight runs through the man, in spite of real sorrows. Nature says: he is my creature, and [in spite of] all his impertinent griefs, he shall be glad with me. . . . Standing on the bare ground, my head bathed by the blithe air, and uplifted into infinite space, all mean egotism vanishes. I become a transparent eye-ball; I am nothing; I see all; the currents of the Universal Being circulate through me; I am part or particle of God.
>
> Ralph Waldo Emerson, *Nature* (1836)

Emerson's experience of nature is an intense and mystical one. It is characteristic of the "transcendentalist" movement. Nature is sacred. Through its contemplation, human beings are freed from worldly distractions and can build a direct connection with God.

Emerson's writings inspired the naturalist John Muir, who created the Sierra Club (a leading conservationist society, still in existence today) to protect California's wilderness.[1] His dream was to free Americans from their rampant materialism. While Emerson thinks that human presence does not soil nature, Muir emphasizes preservation. For him, the only good kind of nature is the true wilderness: "None of Nature's landscapes are ugly so long as they are wild; and much, we can say comfortingly, must always be in great part wild, particularly the sea and the sky, the floods of light from the stars, and the warm, unspoilable heart of the earth, infinitely beautiful, though only dimly visible to the eye of imagination." He then goes on to lament that the Central Valley of California, which was "one bed of golden and purple flowers," is now "plowed and pastured out of existence."[2] Muir dedicated his life to the preservation of nature from the aggression of men and eventually convinced President Theodore Roosevelt to put California's parks under the protection of the federal government.

Transcendentalism elevates wilderness to an absolute: it isn't for sale, it should not be tampered with, and it should be protected. Nowadays, these ideas are in the mainstream. We would probably all agree that building a football stadium or a casino in the Grand Canyon would be evil, even if it created new jobs. We share the intuition that beauty should remain pristine, that it should not be tarnished by economic activities. In this respect, we have all become transcendentalists. This observation applies not only to nature but also to culture. Museums are modern churches: silent and respectful visitors slowly wander between timeless works of art, which they feel privileged to be able to see in person.

Many beautiful places around the world such as museums, cities, and monuments have become sanctuaries. Crowds of tourists make pilgrimages to be inspired by these places. The epitome of this movement is Venice, a city literally being sunk "out of existence" by tourist crowds from around the world. Every year, approximately twenty-six million visitors come to the city, which has a population of some fifty-five thousand on the main islands. The global appetite for beauty, art, and culture is insatiable.

What Price for Access to Beauty?

Yet, beautiful places remain surprisingly affordable. The Greek island of Santorini, overwhelmed by tourist flows in the summers, has set a daily limit of eight thousand individual arrivals in an effort to manage the influx of visitors. Such rationing through quantity, not prices, is a priori an economic heresy. A more natural approach, from an economic viewpoint, would be to increase the price of boarding the island to such a level that only eight thousand tourists feel that visiting Santorini is worth the monetary sacrifice. This way, the locals would still avoid the big crowds, while extracting a larger financial surplus. In practice, however, such an approach, part of the standard economic toolkit, is rarely used. Access to city centers is almost always free, and ticket prices to visit museums are quite low, generating long queues during tourist season. As of 2024, it costs just 22 euros to visit the Louvre in Paris. Forty percent of the nearly eight million visitors who visited the museum in 2022 entered for free because of their age. Seventy percent of the visitors are foreigners (that is, non-French), 18 percent are Americans. Clearly, the price is *not* set to maximize profits, and the museum could apply higher ticket prices, especially to non-EU citizens who have traveled a long way to visit Paris. Museum visitors are in practice quite indifferent to the pricing of entrance tickets, a bit like smokers with cigarette pricing.[3] Still, there is a general reluctance to exploit monuments in a purely mercantilist manner: museum directors want to be the new priests, not the new merchants of the temple . . .

That said, it would be naïve to say that market forces do not play a role in the cultural sector. The art market is brutally competitive, continuously putting a price tag on works of art, old and new. On the supply side, a few names dominate the market, accounting for most of the sales; on the demand side, billionaires and museums battle fiercely to secure iconic pieces that boost their reputation. So, in practice, art, culture, and beauty do have a price, and putting together a museum collection requires large sums of money. It would be delusional to say that art has nothing to do with economics.[4] But, clearly, this relationship is complex and tormented.

To explore the extent to which people are willing to accept the intrusion of economic forces into museums, we asked our international panel of German, US, and French participants about their preferred solution to finance a large museum renovation:

A prominent museum needs to be renovated. The renovation will cost about $500 million.

1. A foreign country proposes to finance the work but in exchange demands that naked statues be dressed or removed. [one-third of the sample]
2. An international foundation proposes to finance the work but in exchange demands that certain works that it considers to be racist be removed. [one-third of the sample]
3. A company in your country proposes to finance the work but in exchange demands to hang advertising posters in the museum. [one-third of the sample]

To what extent do you agree with this initiative?

Each participant is shown one of the three options (at random). Participants who are shown option 3 (financing by a private firm in exchange for advertisement in the museum) tend to strongly agree with the renovation, with an average level of six in France and seven in Germany (out of ten). On both sides of the Atlantic, most participants find it natural to offer counterparties to a firm paying to renovate a museum. They are not shocked and accept the advertising poster.

But this willingness to compromise has limits. Options 1 and 2 are more demanding since the financing party demands control rights over what is exhibited in the museum. In both cases, acceptance is much weaker. Participants offered option 1 (removing or dressing up naked statues) strongly reject the option, with an average level of 2.7 in France and 4.3 in the United States. Overall, people understand that concessions need to be made on museum integrity if the taxpayer does not contribute, but they are not willing to accept just any terms.

What drives the value of beauty, of culture? Is it just a product like any other, like refrigerators or hotel nights? This chapter discusses the nature of our demand for cultural goods, in a broad sense (the arts, but also nature and the sciences). As we hope to convince the reader, there is an old tradition suggesting that we cannot think of culture in purely hedonistic terms, which makes its integration into the economic web more subtle than is the case for standard consumption products. Let us explain.

A Plain Hedonistic View of Art

Indeed, a first approach of culture is to apply the utilitarian framework and argue that the main difference from usual consumption is that cultural goods are public goods, which can be consumed by large groups of people.[5]

The philosopher Peter Singer follows this route and, as a conclusion, criticizes philanthropic donations to museums. He gets to this conclusion by proposing the following thought experiment.[6] A charity receives a big donation, and there are two ways to spend it. Option A is to save one in one thousand people in an African country from going blind. Serious stuff. Option B is to splash the cash on a shiny new museum wing for a million people to enjoy. As a true universalist utilitarian, you should weigh equally the welfare of museum visitors, the utility of citizens of the African country, and your own. Thus, choosing between the two options for others is like choosing for yourself. This allows reformulating the moral dilemma into one that concerns you: Would you rather enjoy a newly renovated museum or dodge a 1-in-1,000 bullet of going blind? Singer is betting you will want to protect your pair of eyes—concluding that museum donations are not moral. We have already seen that this kind of utilitarian reasoning does not capture all moral positions, especially because people are not purely consequentialist (see chapter 2).

Still, we find Singer's thought experiment interesting on another account: it shows that a plain hedonistic view of art consumption does not quite capture the reasons we value art. A museum's value is not just the collection of smiles it sparks. We will try to dig a bit on this intuition, showing how modern economics can integrate it and how a fruitful conceptual dialogue between philosophy and economics can be initiated on this topic.

There will be three moments of our discussion. First, we will discuss how cultural experiences somewhat blur the frontier between effort and leisure, between investment and consumption. Second, we will examine the idea that we might value spending on culture beyond the individual consumer experience that we expect from it. Last, we will go back to a descriptive approach and examine through survey questions how people think about the value of beauty.

Culture, an End in Itself?

Let us take a step back. In the Western philosophical tradition, beauty is an end in itself, something individuals value for its own sake. Beauty generates contemplative pleasure, but to use Kant's language, this pleasure is *disinterested*, it does not satisfy a desire. This sets it apart from hedonistic consumption, where the focus is on deriving pleasure for oneself.[7] In this, the aesthetic experience differs from sensual experiences like eating good food or sitting by a fireplace in the winter. Aesthetic pleasure is not hedonistic; it has a different nature.[8]

According to this tradition, aesthetic judgment is independent of social interactions. It is not affected by how we think others will perceive us. Not everyone agrees with this idealistic view, obviously. For instance, the influential French sociologist Pierre Bourdieu famously came up with a purely cynical view of culture. According to him, behind the curtain of religiosity, high culture has a precise social function: organizing the symbolic domination of higher classes over working classes. Think of museums as the elite's gym for this "soft power." In these places, members of the dominant class can nod to each other, thinking, "Wow, we get this, we're refined." Meanwhile, the working class gets the message loud and clear: we are outsiders, we do not really understand culture, we belong in football stadiums.[9] Empirically, Bourdieu's contribution was to show that museums are mostly attended by the bourgeoisie.[10]

Beyond Consumerism: The Exaltation of "Higher Pleasures"

While Bourdieu's cynical analysis has a kernel of truth (we have a tendency to "show off" culture), it cannot be the entire story. We all feel it by introspection when we experience aesthetic emotions. Sometimes difficult to access, these experiences are "worth it" despite the effort required. They make us grow.

Basic utilitarianism, with its accounting of pleasures and pains, is not well adapted to the description of aesthetic experiences. The two giants of twentieth-century economics, John Maynard Keynes and Joseph Schumpeter, were aligned on this issue. They both had nothing but contempt for the extensive use of Benthamian hedonism, which they found excessively materialistic, focusing people on money-making. For Schumpeter, utilitarianism was a good theory of human behavior concerning what he called "beefsteak issues," but it failed to go much further.[11] Keynes was even more viscerally hostile to utilitarianism and described it, in his memoirs, as "the worm which has been gnawing at the insides of modern civilization and is responsible for its present moral decay." For him, Benthamite calculus was "the most dreadful heresy, perhaps, which has ever gained the ear of a civilized people. Bread and nothing but bread, . . . accumulating at compound interest until it has turned into a stone."[12]

Keynes is so prominent in economics that it is interesting to investigate further what he had in mind. His biography reveals how much he valued the arts above all, in his friendships and his civic initiatives, seeing them as a foundation for civilization. By contrast, he viewed economics and material wealth as just the means to enable higher ends. He often opposed economic forces and aesthetic ends and worried that "the love of money [is] corrosive of community and esthetic values and an encouragement to reckless exploitation of places that should be in the public domain."[13] He believed that a money-making mindset, inherited from Bentham, had become a severe spiritual ailment of capitalist countries, eroding the values of beauty and spiritual matters.

Earlier than Keynes, John Stuart Mill, Bentham's intellectual heir (and son of his personal secretary), struggled with a similar inner conflict between the petty materialism of hedonistic utilitarianism and his own ideals. All his life, he tried to reconcile his fidelity to Benthamian hedonism and his conviction that the quest of pure pleasure is not a valid program for humankind. Like Keynes, Mill found that basic consumerism was not his cup of tea. He thought we should be much more demanding of ourselves: "It is better to be an unsatisfied man than a satisfied pig." But what does this mean, if pleasure is the measure of what is good? Mill did not really solve the issue: he ended up with a clunky patch, modifying Bentham's utilitarian hedonism by drawing a distinction between lower and higher pleasures. Mill argued for a calculation of utility that should give a higher weight to these "pleasures that we owe to intelligence, sensibility, imagination, and moral feelings" and put less weight on the pleasures coming from "pure sensation."[14] Clearly, this hybrid solution is somewhat arbitrary: If they are not based on the intensity of pleasure, who is entitled to decide the weights that should be put in the utility function? The philosopher? The politician? The economist? Of course, one could say, "the people," and often in this book, our solution to the conceptual issues raised by hedonism is to give up on the normative and declare that we should just explore preferences. Still, even within this framework, one is drawn to ask what people value in art, if it isn't pleasure or some of the values we have explored.

Culture and Aspiration: An Investment in Changing Oneself?

A useful notion to understand what is peculiar in our preferences for what Mill called "higher pleasures" is the notion of "aspiration," developed by contemporary philosopher Agnes Callard.[15] Enjoying the arts or the wilderness, or understanding the sciences, is a long and difficult endeavor. It takes patience and persistence. But more specifically, this effort is made *before* we even *know* what we will appreciate. Callard uses the example of a student who is trying to appreciate classical music.

The first few symphonies the student hears require effort more than generating pleasure. High music is not easy; it requires persistence, curiosity, and at first it might feel . . . boring. Its structure and its harmonies differ a lot from what modern ears are used to. Yet the aspiring student persists, spurred on by the feeling that there may be something important to discover. The student's goal is not Bourdieu's social distinction: they do not seek to impress their friends. The aspirant accepts hours of self-denial and concentration, missing out on other pleasures, to attend concerts where they must sit in silence—and this, without really knowing why, since they do not yet know what it is to love this type of music. Callard highlights the opposition between aspiration and ambition. While the ambitious person works (potentially hard) to obtain something they already know, the aspirant works to enjoy a pleasure of which they know almost nothing.

A characteristic of higher pleasures is that they require an up-front investment that we are often reluctant to make. Mill himself had noted the gap between our exalted aspirations and the "infirmity of character" that makes us stumble and sometimes choose the path of least resistance, "though they know it to be the less valuable."[16] In these few lines, Mill described what would eventually become one of the great themes of behavioral economics: our character flaw when it comes to making long-term choices, what modern economists call the *present bias*. It manifests itself when we impulsively make choices we later regret: the well-known temptation to stuff ourselves with peanuts and chips before dinner.

This conflict between a short-term lazy self and a long-term self makes the definition of true preferences more arduous. Normatively, who should take over? Should we encourage people to do what their long-term self wants? Aren't the desires of the short-term self as legitimate? In many situations, it seems intuitively best that the long-term superego should be in charge, as, for instance, in the case of education. The intuition here is that the individual will spend much more time "in the long run" (as an educated adult) than in the "short run" (as a hard-working teenager). So, in the end, it is okay to nudge children to work hard at school. But for culture, this is less obvious: Is educating one's eye to painting worth it in the age of video games? Should children be forced to learn how to enjoy the music of Arnold Schoenberg in the age of Taylor Swift?

Thus, consensus in behavioral economics is to normatively put much more weight on the aspirations of the long-term self, the one who will regret giving in to the easy path and would like to follow an ambitious or courageous behavior (morally, humanly, professionally). In this sense, behavioral economists follow Mill's precepts: it is our aspirations, not our actual behavior, that should define our true preferences. And some degree of paternalism may, in this case, be required; we will return to this issue below.

Culture as a Public Good

So far, we have discussed higher pleasures from the viewpoint of the individual only. But culture is not just a personal affair; it is a collective one. We care about it even if we are not directly exposed to it. It is important to us that it is "somewhere out there."

Consider the National Park Service (legacy of Muir and the transcendentalists): it enjoys large popular support, even from people who do not visit the parks. A 2019 bill to spend $6.5 billion to improve the national parks won the approval of eight out of ten Americans.[17] This number can be contrasted with the fraction of Americans actually visiting national parks: currently, about 55 percent of Americans have visited a national park in the past three years.[18] So in apparent contradiction with utilitarianism, individuals support the preservation of natural heritage, even if they do not get to enjoy it much personally.

Another example is the worldwide emotion created by the fire at Notre Dame Cathedral in April 2019. In just a few days, nearly $1 billion was pledged globally to help rebuild the cathedral. Among these donors, many do not often, if ever, visit the cathedral (much less pray there). So there is in our relationship to culture and nature something that goes beyond our direct enjoyment of it. This is important, as it implies that the value of artistic and scientific production cannot be measured by the propensity of the population to pay for concert, museum, or movie tickets alone. To speak like an economist, we can say that on these matters, people's observable transactions do not fully "reveal preferences."

To further analyze this insight, we designed a question in the spirit of Peter Singer's thought experiment, but this time emphasizing cultural and natural heritage. We asked US participants:

> Federal spending on National Parks and on museums such as the Smithsonian Institution is about $4 billion annually. Some people argue that these public funds could be better spent by giving medications to poor populations in the US or fighting opioid addiction.
>
> On a scale of 1 to 5, how much do you agree?

Only 42 percent of the respondents agree with the idea of reallocating government money from American heritage (the Smithsonian) or nature (national parks) toward the poor. Centrists are more likely to agree with the reallocation of federal funds than the most conservative or liberal respondents. It may be because centrists are more sensitive to technocratic utilitarian calculus and think the value of a life is higher than that of an American artifact or landscape.

The other interesting observation is that such an opinion is only partially explained by museum attendance or park visits. Among those who rarely or never go to the museum (their last visit was more than five years ago, or never), 31 percent disagree (strongly or somewhat) with the reallocation of funds away from the Smithsonian. This suggests that there is a large number of respondents who care enough about heritage that they are willing to spend tax dollars on its preservation, even though they barely enjoy it directly.

Cultural and Natural Heritage: Two Logics

So, the hedonic utilitarian approach only takes us so far. There is a collective dimension to our commitment to art, science, and nature. We honor culture even if we don't plan to directly enjoy it much ourselves.

We subsidize the protection of wilderness even when we rarely hike in the forests and parks. Why? There are two logics potentially at play here: *transmissive* and *preservative*.

The first logic is that of heritage and transmission *to other humans* (future generations, other nations). Arts and sciences are our legacy to the next generations, our communication to all of humanity. We care for what our time bequeaths and are ready to finance science, culture, or the wilderness. We find here something close to the logic of altruism: we put some weight on how others (potentially unborn people) will feel in the future. According to Ronald Dworkin,[19] intellectual heritage is essential because it provides a common language for the community and developmental opportunities for the individual. This heritage can wither away, due to lack of maintenance or prolonged confinement in the ivory towers of academia. The duty of each generation is to "leave this structure as rich as it found it" to the next generation. It looks like we internalize this duty to keep these common goods alive.

This leads us to the second logic behind our nonselfish commitment to nature and culture, which is conceptually more daring, and was also proposed by Dworkin. It is the idea that we care about artistic output or nature to exist *independently* of the joy it will bring to our descendants or fellow humans. We want it to survive us. For example, you might care that the statues of Easter Island keep existing and looking at the sky, just for their own sake, not because they might be a source of utility for others. Or another example: imagine for a moment that the entirety of Russian literature suddenly vanishes. According to Dworkin (the example is from him), the tragedy here would not simply be the loss for the readers (present and future) of Tolstoy. The real tragedy would be the disappearance of a universe that was alive in our brains. Raymond Bradbury's *Fahrenheit 451* provides an illustration of this logic. The novel paints a totalitarian society that systematically confiscates and burns all the books (on the grounds that the stories they contain can be offensive). Book lovers are a clandestine group of humans who live on the margins of society. To save literature from destruction, each book lover devotes their life to accurately memorizing one book.

Their goal is not to spread the book content—they are not allowed to do this—but merely to make sure it does not go into oblivion.

It is certainly about nature that the conservation viewpoint resonates the most deeply: we value that planet Earth remains a lively ecosystem, irrespective of whether humans are here to witness it. So, it is about not just preserving scenic trails for future generations of hikers but also valuing our planet as an irreplaceable treasure, fighting for its intrinsic right to thrive. More and more, ecological consciousness values biodiversity for its own sake (species have a right to flourish) rather than for utilitarian reasons (such as avoiding systemic risk to our food ecosystem). Consider a scenario in which a business venture threatens the survival of a rare plant species. Let us say this species doesn't serve humans, doesn't play a vital role in its ecosystem, and isn't exactly a feast for the eyes. Given its vegetative nature, it doesn't have feelings. Yet, even with all this "nonutilitarian" context, we might feel compelled to make sacrifices to protect this species, just for the sake of maintaining its existence.

This commitment also applies to fundamental science, including mathematics. A materialistic argument for supporting research in basic science is based on the possibility of future (often unexpected) technological applications. But basic science also has value for itself. In the early nineteenth century, mathematicians were not obsessed with applications. For instance, nineteenth-century mathematician Carl Jacobi wrote in a letter to his colleague Adrien-Marie Legendre: "The sole purpose of science is the honor of the human mind."[20] In other words, research in mathematics cannot be reduced to its usefulness. It has value for its own sake, like poetry or music.

Educating for Culture

To sum up, our preferences for culture, the sciences, or nature walk on two legs. The first is a form of sophisticated utilitarianism inspired by Mill's notion of higher pleasures. The second is a common heritage, intellectual and environmental, that must be maintained and transmitted, as an end in itself. These two logics legitimize government intervention, in other words, a cultural policy.

Let us start with the educational component of cultural policy. John Stuart Mill, who was no cheerleader of paternalism, strongly believed in the importance of education in combating our tendency to indulge in common pleasures. Exposing youth to cultural goods, teaching notions that are not just professionally useful but also intellectually nourishing, was according to him the only way to grow a taste for art and culture. The value of our education is not just the sum of our future salaries. Exposure to human knowledge and to the arts is integral to the accomplishment of what Mill called the "plan of life," the construction of the self that is both the right and the duty of the autonomous individual. An education in the liberal arts as well as the sciences achieves that objective. Practical knowledge that can be used in the job market does not.

If liberal intellectuals, in the tradition of Mill, are comfortable with educational policies, they are generally less excited by the idea of government-based protection of culture. This is often because they fear the emergence of a class of cultural apparatchiks with little democratic legitimacy. For the nineteenth-century French essayist Frédéric Bastiat (famous for his economic thought experiments illustrating the virtues of free markets), the worker should not be forced by the State to pay for the artist's salary.[21] The novelist and Nobel laureate Mario Vargas Llosa feels comfortable saying that "the threat to Flaubert and Debussy does not come from the dinosaurs of Jurassic Park but from the bunch of petty demagogues and chauvinists who talk about culture as if it were a mummy that cannot be removed from its room because exposure to fresh air would cause it to disintegrate."[22]

These visceral reactions notwithstanding, since the intellectual and natural heritage has the attributes of a public good (we consume it collectively), there is room for the government to solve a collective action problem (one might tend to free-ride on the others regarding the production of such goods, even though we all care about them). Further, we value transmitting it to others even if we do not expect to consume it ourselves (the transmission view) and value maintaining its existence (the conservation view). On that basis, it is possible to develop a liberal conception of the role of the state, foundations, or NGOs as curators of nature, the arts, and sciences. This is the role played by the Smithsonian Institution in the United States, but other countries in the world have a more active, state-level cultural policy.[23]

Eliciting Preferences about Beauty and Heritage

If there is a role for the nonprofit sector in curating our heritage, this role must, however, be disciplined by the preferences of citizens. Vargas Llosa is right: a classic drift of these policies—it certainly happens in our own country—consists of giving civil servants and their cliques privileged positions to define what is good or bad art, what should become a piece of heritage that deserves protection, and what should be allowed to go to oblivion. While some degree of paternalism is sensible in education, it is harder to justify with adult citizens.

How easy is it to know people's aspirations? One option, which economists like, is the "method of revealed preferences." We observe how much people pay for sciences and the arts and how much of it they consume and use this to figure out how much they care about it. This would be a sensible approach to understanding culture and nature on a utilitarian basis, and this approach has some merit. Yet, it runs against two limitations that we have discussed in this section. First, pure utilitarian concerns do not fully account for our aspiration to high culture. We may aspire to spend our evening reading a Russian novel and yet end up watching a true crime show on Netflix. Another wedge between aspirations and actions comes from the training required to appreciate beauty and culture. Second, many of us value the preservation of our cultural heritage, without directly being consumers of it. For these two reasons, the method of revealing preferences would give us the wrong answer to the question: What do people really care about?

The surveys we have run, and whose results we describe throughout this book, have a higher chance of being able to capture these subtle aspirations. A downside of these surveys—like any other survey—is that people may not always act on their answers. But this can also be a strength: it suggests that people report their aspirations, what they think would be the "right" answer. It is essential to make respondents consider trade-offs when answering by not asking, "Would you want a museum for free in your neighborhood?" but rather "Would you be willing to build a museum at the expense of not renovating the football stadium?" Highlighting trade-offs is an important step toward obtaining meaningful answers. Assuming we can do this, it is a way to inform policy about people's cultural aspirations.

8
Companies

Big business has a bad reputation. Over the past fifty years, the fraction of Americans who place "very little confidence or none" in big business has grown from 29 percent to 41 percent.[1] One of the reasons is that people perceive firms as imperfect moral agents, which are dealing with ethical trade-offs all the time. They can lower production costs by shipping production to countries allowing child labor. They can aggressively market painkillers, at the cost of rising levels of addiction and overdoses. They can promote teenage use of social media, even though it may lead to depression and suicide. All this is legal, of course. Firms can claim their economic mission is to maximize profits. When they undertake legal yet harmful activities, they do so not out of evil but out of simple greed, which benefits shareholders. And often, other "stakeholders" also benefit from corporate greed: employees of more profitable firms are paid higher wages, and customers get better and cheaper products. Such tensions between profits and morals thus raise uncomfortable questions. Are we, as shareholders, customers, or employees, willing to pay the price of corporate virtue? Should firms exercise self-restraint and uphold certain values? If so, who should define their ethics? The goal of this chapter is to explore these questions.

The Russia Exodus

Let us start with an example of such corporate dilemmas. After the February 2022 Russian invasion of Ukraine, multinationals responded to calls from various activists demanding strict boycotts of Russia. Nine months into the war, more than one thousand firms had pledged to shut down their Russian operations.[2] Some of these plans were partial, and others were complete. For some firms, withdrawal would be permanent, but for most, it would be temporary.

What was the ethical thing to do? One question is whether corporate withdrawals have a real impact. Take the example of an oil company that owns a refinery in Russia. Leaving Russia means selling the plant to a local investor. If the buyer pays a fair price for it, the transaction is neither a punishment nor a gift. The oil company receives an amount that compensates it for the loss of future cash flows. The refinery will continue to operate and pay dividends to the new owner. In the present situation, however, there are presumably few Russian buyers. It is thus likely that the foreign company will not receive much compensation, if any. Withdrawing from Russia may then imply a quasi-donation to a Putin affiliate. In fact, from a consequentialist perspective, the only good action would be to destroy the refinery before leaving.

Here is another example of a thorny moral dilemma. Imagine that a global fast-food chain shuts down all its restaurants in Russia. This will imply that it stops paying its employees, who will become jobless in a country at war. Isn't this disloyal to them? Can they be held responsible for what their leader does? Exiting Russia is not *obviously* the right thing to do. It depends on whether the firms' stockholders are deontological or consequentialist. Deontological investors want to do what is right, as a matter of principles. They prefer to have nothing to do with Russia and to keep their hands clean, irrespective of the consequences. Consequentialist investors want to maximize the good, abstracting away from principles. For instance, they may choose to have the firm stay in Russia, pay its employees, and donate the profits to Ukraine. Or alternatively, give a generous severance package to employees and burn down the restaurants.

The second ambiguity is whether acting morally is costly or not. One view (the "moral firm" view) would be that the owners of these firms are acting out of compassion. They care not just about their materialistic well-being but also about values. Such moral firms are willing to sacrifice part of their profits by exiting from Russia. The other view (the "win-win" view) is that acting morally is good for business, so there is no trade-off to consider. Firms need to preserve their global reputations with customers, employees, and governments. They need to avoid negative media buzz. As a result, exiting Russia might be a win for profits. This argument was often invoked by CEOs deciding to withdraw from Russia. When it is profitable, who would disagree with doing the right thing?

A third, related question is governance. In these announcements, shareholders were in most cases not consulted. The decision to withdraw from Russia was made by the managers of these firms, likely after discussions with the board of directors, which represents shareholders. But there was no formal stockholder vote. Recall that in US common law, managers' only duty is to maximize the interest of stockholders. This leads to two possibilities. If these decisions increase firm profits (if the "win-win" view holds), executives acted according to their mandate. They were maximizing profits by being moral. If, however, pulling out of Russia hurts profits (if the "moral firm" view holds), then managers were in breach of their duty. They did not have the mandate to do this. This raises questions about the decision-making process. Should management's role be to maximize stockholder profit, or should management be given a different mandate?

In this chapter, we will explore the last two questions: the cost of corporate virtue, and the governance of the moral firm. But before going there, it helps to start with the mainstream economic doctrine. Faithful to Adam Smith's separation between morals and markets, economists predominantly think that companies should stay away from moral trade-offs. Instead, they argue that firms should focus on maximizing profits and leave all the complex moral thinking to regulators and politicians. Let us start by examining the merits of this doctrine.

The Friedman Doctrine

Written in 1970 by Milton Friedman, "The Social Responsibility of Business Is to Increase Its Profits" is probably one of the most influential newspaper opinion pieces ever written.[3] The website Google Scholar counts about twenty-seven thousand citations as of the time of this writing (much more than most academic economists' entire body of work). Every year, around two thousand new academic articles and economic analyses cite it. Saying that this is a foundational text is an understatement.

Friedman wrote this opinion piece as a response to the growing movement of "corporate social responsibility," which in the late 1960s argued that business should be concerned not only with profits but also with "providing employment, eliminating discrimination, avoiding pollution and whatever else." In his view, this movement was misguided and based on loose reasoning. Friedman then embarked on listing several arguments for why this is the case.

His main argument is that a moral corporation would face crippling governance deficiencies. First, its managers have not been trained for this role: they have been trained to create, finance, and market the company's products, but they are not experts in complicated economic and moral trade-offs beyond this. Friedman states, "I have been impressed time and again by the schizophrenic character of many businessmen. They are capable of being extremely far-sighted and clear-headed in matters that are internal to their businesses. They are incredibly short-sighted and muddle-headed in matters that are outside their businesses but affect the possible survival of business in general." For instance, managers who would want to help fight inflation by moderating their companies' prices are not macroeconomists. Their good intentions will backfire. They ignore that inflation is triggered by an expansion of the money supply beyond their control. Thus, even if they refrain from increasing their own prices, others will increase theirs. Their own products may end up becoming unprofitable to make: since costs increase with inflation, they make a dent in firm profits. This discourages shareholders from investing. Product supply will shrink, creating more inflation.

The second issue is one of accountability. Managers are agents of shareholders. They are not spending their own money and have no legitimacy to use the company's resources to further a cause (however worthy) that they believe in. Shareholders set the company's goal and hold managers accountable for their actions. Classic, for-profit corporations at least have a clear objective: managers are evaluated on their success at generating present and future profits. Expecting managers to deal with moral trade-offs opens the door to incompetence hiding behind a smokescreen of fuzzy corporate intentions. We will return to this challenge at the end of this chapter.

Third, dealing with moral trade-offs is complicated and messy. Each one of us has our own morality; disagreement on what should be done is the norm. This is why the political process exists. It is far from perfect (to say the least), but it is legitimate because we all agree that politics is the place where these complex tensions may be resolved. The slowness of the government to act is a feature, not a bug, according to Friedman: inaction simply means a lack of consensus about collective actions and goals. Companies have different roles: selling detergent and telephones, not deciding what is right or preventing harm. This separation of roles is commonly understood, anchored in tradition, and therefore legitimate. Any other arrangement, according to Friedman, would blur the lines and lead to abuse of power and dilution of responsibilities.

Back to the Separation of Money and Morals

In the end, corporate morality is so impractical that Friedman—for a reason very different from Smith—advocates for a strict separation of morality and profits. Of course, the company's owners (its shareholders) may feel they have a certain responsibility toward society and should be free to do what they think is right. But the most effective way of doing this is for the company to generate profits. Then, shareholders are free to use the profits they benefit from to defend their preferred causes. Here is the argument Friedman's article is famous for:

> The stockholders or the customers or the employees could separately spend their own money on the particular action if they wished to do so. The executive is exercising a distinct "social responsibility," rather than serving as an agent of the stockholders or the customers, or the employees, only if he spends the money in a different way than they would have spent it.

There we have it. In the end, Friedman's argument is a moral one, based on individual liberties. Everyone has their own value system, determining priorities that most deserve their sacrifice. If companies focus on profits and distribute them, shareholders can choose the cause each one of them wants to support: this preserves moral autonomy. If, on the contrary, the company, however well governed, chooses one moral objective, all shareholders are forced into supporting this cause. Of course, individual rights can be subordinated to the collective good, but only the government can enforce this—it has the "monopoly of legitimate violence." No private entity has the right to limit individual liberties.

When Goodness Helps Profits

In many situations, corporate moral decisions do not entail a trade-off: doing the right thing is sometimes good for business. Legal scholar Lucian Bebchuk calls this type of reasoning "instrumental stakeholderism."[4] Making stakeholders (customers, the community, employees, and so on) happy, even if it costs a little, may be in the interest of shareholders. For Bebchuk, such situations do not pose a challenge to Friedman's view that managers should aim at maximizing profits. Giving an extra week of paid vacation or long maternity leave may help attract the most talented young college graduates. Sourcing inputs responsibly may appeal to millennial consumers who are concerned with the environment. Being more environmentally conscious than what current standards require might give a leading edge if one anticipates that regulations will become tighter in the near term. Morality can be seen in such cases as an instrument for (current and long-term) profits, not necessarily as a goal for its own sake. Friedman had of course thought about this: "It may well be in the long-run interest of a corporation that is a major employer in a small community to devote resources to providing amenities to that community or to improving its government. That may make it easier to attract desirable employees, it may reduce the wage bill or lessen losses from pilferage and sabotage or have other worthwhile effects."[5]

In a recent book, economist Alex Edmans develops a similar intuition, but he thinks it only works when firms *do not* focus on shareholder profit maximization.[6] He takes the example of a company investing in a gym for its employees. The goal is clearly to make employees happy and hopefully to increase the company's bottom line. But a profit-focused company would need to first measure the increased profits obtained from happier employees and then compare them to the cost of building the gym—a hopeless task. A better approach, Edmans argues, is to shift firms' focus to *social* value ("grow the pie"). Such a mindset creates trust in the organization; it makes it easier to elicit collaboration from consumers and employees. And, eventually, the firm's owners will benefit from a larger pie. The paradox of Edmans's proposal is that the only way to really maximize profits is to maximize *not* profits but rather social value. Of course, managers should still be held accountable for their mistakes. Edmans requires that the company's purpose should be clear, communication needs to be transparent, and the metrics of success be broad but precise.

Another vocal champion of stakeholder capitalism is Rebecca Henderson in *Reimagining Capitalism in a World of Fire*.[7] Like many before her, Henderson criticizes the short-termism of corporations, the "cost-cutting" managerial mindset. By being so focused on not leaving money on the table, by neglecting to think about the future, managers forget that treating stakeholders well improves long-term corporate performance. This view has its merits, but it does not really "reimagine" capitalism; it is more of a management guidebook that is adapted to modern capitalism. It teaches managers to make money by tackling the big problems faced by our societies, such as climate change. Asking themselves what is good for society is a way for managers to identify activities that will thrive in the coming decades.

Customers' and Employees' Moral Concerns

A particularly powerful group of stakeholders who can impose their values on a firm are the customers. Some of us are old enough to remember the outrage against Nike in the early 1990s after an activist reported on the company's labor practices in Indonesia (low wages, child labor, appalling work conditions). Consumers do value the fact that a good is produced with higher ethical standards. A large literature in marketing research shows that consumers declare themselves willing to pay a sizable premium for products that are Fair Trade certified. The question, however, is whether this is the case in real life.

To address this, a team of political scientists has partnered with a large US grocery chain based in New England.[8] Stores in this chain had bins for bulk coffee. Stores had to place neutral or "Fair Trade" labels on the bulk bins, in a random fashion. In this convincing exercise, the researchers found that sales of Fair Trade coffee were larger by about 10 percent, for a given price. As it turns out, the willingness to pay for this label is higher for customers buying more expensive beans to start with ("French Roast" as opposed to "Coffee Blend"); in another experiment the authors found that increasing the price of Fair Trade French Roast by 9 percent has no effect on demand. To put it simply, this research shows that, at least among more affluent New Englanders, people are willing to pay higher prices for well-sourced coffee. To attract or retain such customers, a profit-maximizing firm needs to manufacture or source prosocial products.

Employees are also important stakeholders and sometimes force companies to behave morally. First, employees are, like everyone else, altruistic. They want to work for a company that takes care of its community, the environment, and so on. Shareholders in turn benefit from this: employees will be easier to attract, will work harder, and will accept lower pay at a company they love. Consistent with this intuition, a large literature in economics documents the benefits, in terms of pay, effort, and retention, of corporate social responsibility.[9] For instance, looking at firm payroll data under the microscope, Philipp Krüger and his coauthors show that environmentally responsible companies can afford to pay their workers less (some 3 to 4 percent less, depending on the measure).[10] Of course, this is again a situation in which companies do well by doing good.

The Limits of Instrumental Stakeholderism

Even if workers in socially responsible firms are more motivated and more effective, it does not automatically imply that these firms are more profitable. It naturally depends on the cost of being responsible. Take the example of a food company. By committing to a new charitable initiative designed to help farmers, this company is able to attract young, well-educated, Gen Z employees who are both cheaper and more motivated. Our hypothetical food company would expect a cost reduction of, say, $100 million per year. Of course, this new initiative is costly (if it were a profitable project, this entire discussion would be useless, as the company would undertake it in any case). If the charitable initiative costs, say, $80 million, then virtue pays: the company will launch the project and expect to earn another $20 million per year. But if this cost is larger than $100 million per year, then shareholders will, on net, lose.

This simple arithmetic raises the issue of who profits from corporate responsibility. In our example, employees' concerns for sustainable agriculture lead them to indirectly subsidize shareholders' profits.

Realizing this, they may bargain for higher salaries, thereby reducing the gain shareholders may expect. Overall, even if there are gains from corporate social responsibility, it is not entirely clear who will cash them in.

To approach this issue, we have posed a version of this question to our survey participants in the United States, Germany, and France. We set the stage with a company starting a charitable initiative. Depending on the participant (and on a random basis), the initiative is paid for by employees, shareholders, or a mix of both. We then ask how much they support it.

> A multinational is proposing to launch a volunteer-based activity for developing countries. It will supply methods to help farmers there. This activity will not be profitable for the company, but it will be very useful to farmers in these countries.
>
> - To fund this new activity, the company will freeze all salaries for 3 years. [one-third of the sample]
> - To fund this new activity, the company will freeze all salaries and shareholder dividends for 3 years. [one-third of the sample]
> - To fund this new activity, the company will freeze shareholder dividends for 3 years. [one-third of the sample]
>
> On a scale of 1 to 10, to what extent do you agree with this initiative?

Unsurprisingly, participants strongly support the initiative, with an average level of 6.5 across countries, when it is 100 percent financed by shareholders. As soon as employees are required to chip in, support plummets. If the company needs to freeze salaries to finance the entire initiative, the average agreement level drops to 4.7. If shareholders share part of the burden, the average goes up to 5, still well below the level reached when shareholders foot the entire bill.

Overall, this suggests that participants feel shareholders should pay for the charitable initiative. Of course, this outcome may depend on aspects of our design. First, this is a very specific project (helping farmers in developing countries), and other projects might garner more enthusiasm. Second, it is the company that decides on the project, not the employees. Thus, survey participants do not feel that they own the decision. Third, the project involves farmers in developing countries, not local farmers.

To wrap up this discussion, let us just say that, even if corporate social responsibility has benefits for shareholders, it also has costs. In some situations, these costs outweigh the benefits, and instrumental stakeholderism will not work. This is apparent in the question we asked: participants want shareholders to bear all of the cost of the charitable action.

A study focusing on customers, not employees, finds similar results among eBay vendors.[11] Vendors on the platform can decide to give a fraction of their sales price to charities. Researchers have found that, in this case, pledging to give out one dollar per product sold leads to an increased willingness to pay by about 25 cents. Thus, giving one dollar does not cost a full dollar to the vendor, but it still costs 75 cents. As in our question about employees, it is impossible for an eBay vendor in this study to use charitable behavior to increase profits.

Questioning Corporate Sincerity

The instrumentalization of goodness can backfire even more when it sheds doubt on the sincerity of the firm. If the company pretends to be moral but clearly does so out of interest, this can trigger distrust. For instance, when employees choose a company, they are not just looking at their compensation. They are also looking for signs that the company will be a good fit for their personal goals, that it will provide them with a good career path, that hard work will be compensated, that the work environment is not toxic, and so on. This can be achieved by companies that are not 100 percent profit-oriented, companies that are willing to leave a few bucks on the table to keep their workers happy. By behaving morally, companies send that signal and are better at attracting and retaining employees. But of course, employees are not naïve; they will require that signal to be trustworthy: this makes it harder to instrumentalize moral behavior to make more money. If the commitment to social responsibility is not genuine, stakeholders will naturally question the company's motives. Will the company remain altruistic when doing so is no longer in its financial interest? An opportunistic company might not think twice about taking harsh measures when it becomes profitable to do so, such as ramping up work pressures, halting promotions, or downsizing staff.

Experimental research documents several typical situations where instrumental goodness does not work. Economists Lea Cassar and Stephan Meier set up a field experiment in which an Italian firm crowdsources a simple job: inventing three marketing slogans for its English website for a baseline payment.[12] Employees then can write additional slogans. First, the researchers simply show that classic financial incentives do indeed motivate workers: They propose an additional payment (smaller than the baseline). Making this additional payment *conditional* on workers writing more slogans triggers a lot more effort: this is not surprising but a kind of "smell test" that the experiment runs normally. In a second step, they transform this additional payment into a charity donation (so workers write the additional slogans to make this donation). The surprising result here is that, in this case, making the donation *conditional* on workers writing more slogans *reduces* their effort: they become *less* likely to write additional slogans, and they write fewer of them. Using charity donations as an incentive backfires, most likely because workers see the firm as taking advantage of their altruism. Along the same line, Matthew Amengual and Evan Apfelbaum find that, when organizations want their employees to embrace behaviors that are both prosocial and instrumental to the organization, the best way to get them on board is by emphasizing the instrumental side of things and to not mention the prosocial one.[13] Emphasizing instrumental reasons just feels more genuine. By contrast, the prosocial motive sounds hypocritical. Many of us who have stayed in hotels that bombard their customers with flashy messages that it is better for the planet if you use only one towel for all your stay might relate to this finding. Being taken for a fool is unpleasant.

Recently, the management literature has insisted on the negative effects of "greenwashing"—situations where firms are caught exaggerating and misrepresenting their environmental efforts. Claims of environmental commitments can easily backfire if they turn out to be inauthentic and can create hostility from all stakeholders.[14] One notable example of greenwashing that led to significant backlash is the case of Volkswagen's "Clean Diesel" scandal.[15] Volkswagen, a major automobile manufacturer, promoted its diesel-powered cars as environmentally friendly. However, it was revealed that the company had been instrumentalizing not only the environmental consciousness of its customers but also the emissions testing process itself, with a software program activating a low pollution mode during testing phases. When the truth came to light in 2015, it ignited a scandal that led to outrage from customers who had purchased these vehicles under the assumption that they were environmentally conscious choices. The company lost more than 40 percent in value.

To summarize these last few pages, the case for instrumental stakeholderism is theoretically sound, but it faces strong limitations in practice as it only applies when there is no trade-off between morals and profits. The foundation for ethical behavior that it provides is fragile and does not cover the many situations where the financial rewards from making stakeholders happy (be it consumers or employees) do not outweigh the costs of acting more virtuously. Besides, instrumentalizing compassion may raise doubts about the sincerity of the firm and may backfire due to people's distaste for hypocrisy: organizations that want to benefit from stakeholders' moral sympathy need to convince them that they are sincere and not just trying to instrumentalize morals for profits.

Nonprofit Organizations: Dropping the Instrumental Motive

One way for organizations to convince stakeholders they are sincerely caring about social externalities is to drop the for-profit motive altogether. That way, the suspicion of being exploited vanishes. People cooperate more easily with an organization they believe to be candid in its social commitments.

This might be one of the reasons why a large fraction of firms, even of the US economy, consists of nonprofits. Nonprofits are prevalent in industries such as health care and education and also present in banking and retail (via cooperatives, credit unions, and thrifts). As of 2016, nonprofit employment in the United States (excluding cooperatives and credit unions) was about 10.2 percent of total private employment (thus excluding government employees).[16] For example, the universities we work for, both reasonably well-functioning institutions, have no shareholders and do not seek to maximize profits. Their objectives are fuzzier. For instance, MIT's mission statement is to "advance knowledge and educate students in science, technology, and other areas of scholarship that will best serve the nation and the world in the 21st century." The institute seeks "to develop in each member of the MIT community the ability and passion to work wisely, creatively, and effectively for the betterment of humankind."[17] This is a worthy objective, but one that can be understood in many different ways. One could argue that such objectives are too broadly defined to ensure proper governance of higher education institutions, yet MIT is successful at attracting the best students in the world and at producing cutting-edge research.

Why is this? There are two reasons. First, universities are competing for students, for research funds, for professors. Competition, as with classic for-profit corporations, ensures that nonprofits run a tight ship. It is the great enforcer of good governance. Second, nonprofits have stakeholders that have incentives similar to those of shareholders: they benefit, financially or otherwise, from the fact that the institution is well run. Big donors prefer to invest in well-run charities. Well-run universities pay faculty and staff better and provide more funding for research. Altruistic employees prefer to take on more and larger projects, enlarge their group of colleagues, help more people, and so on. All these motivations can successfully replace the for-profit motive because they induce a concern for not wasting money.

In health care and education, and to some extent in banking, another argument in favor of nonprofits kicks in: consumption in these sectors needs to be highly personalized, and the seller of the product knows better than the buyer what is fit for them. Sick persons do not know much about their illnesses or the appropriate treatment. They might not know someone with a similar condition. Students do not know what they need to learn. This makes it important in these industries that the provider is ethical and not just trying to sell expensive products. By not being profit-oriented, education and health care institutions send a credible signal that they have the welfare of their clients at heart. Economist Sabrina Howell and her coauthors have recently provided convincing tests of this view. They have assembled data on nursing homes, higher education, and local newspapers.[18] They find that every time, when private equity investors (investors that care more about profits) take control of firms in these sectors, the quality of service deteriorates. Such a finding is consistent with the idea that a stronger profit objective reduces these firms' altruistic concerns for their employees. Overall, that banks, hospitals, universities, and retailers have this structure is not surprising, since the information gap between sellers and buyers in these industries is important. Buyers who fear abuse may prefer nonprofit suppliers.

Beyond Instrumental Goodness

Now, it is evident that the economy cannot solely depend on nonprofit organizations. If anything, the history of communist economies gives some evidence that a system devoid of the profit motive is not appealing. In numerous countries globally, state-owned enterprises have demonstrated less efficiency and innovation compared to their private counterparts. The drive to generate profits is a potent incentive for innovation, pushing for the creation of top-notch products aimed at reaching the widest consumer base possible. So we are back to for-profit firms: Is there a case to be made for for-profit firms to become moral beyond the instrumental motive?

We have just seen that it is not easy: people suspect the firm might just be doing marketing, that it might be trying to exploit their feelings. Still, in the last part of this chapter, we will develop arguments in this direction. We will address situations where morality decreases profits (so that there is no more concern regarding instrumentalization).

Let's start by investigating what people aspire to. Survey participants tend to think that firms should not just maximize profits. In our representative US survey, 69 percent of the respondents agree with the statement that "a moral duty of firms towards society is to limit wage inequality among their employees" (while only 15 percent disagree). Of course, the political divide is significant: 89 percent of the more liberal respondents agree with the moral duty, against only 43 percent of the conservatives. Still, this moral view of the firm is pervasive in all segments of the population.

To double-check that this is how people think, we formulated a more concrete question that explicitly highlights the trade-off between employee welfare and shareholder profits:

> In a large company, a manager considers the decision to close an unproductive plant. Keeping this plant open costs $[1/10/100] million to the owners of the firm every year. If the plant is closed, employees will lose their jobs (there is no vacant position for them in the company). Most of these employees are more than 50 years old, so it will not be easy for them to find a job.
>
> What should the manager do? Keep the employees or fire them?

We randomize the cost of keeping the employees: respondents are split into three groups, with the cost of keeping employees varying from $1 to $100 million per year. Overall, 72 percent think the company should keep the employees, and this percentage does not depend on the cost. Of course, it varies across political leanings, but even among self-declared conservatives, 56 percent think the company should not fire the employees (85 percent of the liberals). Thus, our survey participants do not think that companies should just maximize profits, and the answer seems strongly driven by political values.

As we argued in our discussion of Friedman's 1970 article, such a view is clearly at odds with what most mainstream economists believe (and, as one of us noticed, at odds with what finance students think). One possibility is that this view is self-interested: our respondents may picture themselves as older employees, more than as the anonymous shareholders, who stand to gain from the layoffs. We do not think this is the entire story, for essentially three reasons. First, even among higher-income respondents (above $110,000 of self-reported income), a majority still choose to keep the employees (64 percent). This opinion is even more prevalent among the most educated part of our participants (68 percent among graduates of four-year colleges). Second, education and income predict opinions much less than Jonathan Haidt's measures of moral values (compassion, fairness, loyalty, sanctity, and authority). Third, our sample is representative of the US population distribution by age and political leanings. It thus contains a significant fraction of voters who are not old.

The Case for the Moral Firm

If people disagree with economists so much, why is that so? The first thing to note is that there is general agreement (even among economists) that the common good could in principle benefit significantly from firms having some "moral concerns." The reason is the existence of externalities (positive and negative) that firms do not consider if profits are their sole compass. When maximizing profits, firms can do a lot of damage to society: in this case, what is good for shareholders is not what is good for society. For instance, shareholders in the survey question posed above do not take into account the fact that the (hypothetical) employees will never find a job if they are fired. Their productivity is low (they were making products that sell at a loss), but it is not zero.

However, even though economists understand that unbridled profit maximization may hurt society, they would still maintain, like Milton Friedman, that dealing with this problem is the role of the government. Instead of expecting self-restraint from companies, it is much more effective to rely on a strong regulator that will force companies to take these problems into account. And this is not a pure utopia: actual regulations do try to penalize socially harmful behavior. Companies that fire their workers are often (directly or indirectly) taxed on layoffs. Banks—especially since the 2008 financial crisis—are regulated to avoid excess lending and bankruptcies. Manufacturers are prevented from polluting the environment through a mixture of taxes, mandatory disclosure, and regulation.

The limit of this argument, however, is that in many situations, firms can inflict significant harm on society while remaining well within the boundaries of the law. Many examples come to mind where such harm could eventually be repaired but at great cost to society (potentially larger than the benefits to these firms' shareholders). For instance, most banks were compliant with regulations before 2008, even those that needed a public bail-out once the crisis erupted. Even if their shareholders cashed in a few hundreds of billions of dollars in extra dividends, the cost of the financial crisis was much larger than this.

Another example: many experts link social media to teenage depression, a problem that will be hard to solve going forward. The number of teenage girls injuring themselves has doubled since 2010 (so that the population most exposed to social media has experienced a sharp deterioration of mental health). Additionally, there is a strong correlation between social media use and depression, but only for girls.[19] Thus, even though social media's activities are 100 percent legal, there is suspicion they may put the mental health of an entire generation in danger.

In health care, Purdue Pharma has been condemned multiple time for igniting the opioid epidemic that has caused the deaths of hundreds of thousands of Americans (though the company's shareholders seem to remain quite wealthy and have not faced any criminal charges at the time of this writing). Another, slightly more ambiguous example is the chemical company DuPont, which made the calculated decision to release a toxic chemical (C8, used to make Teflon) into the Ohio River, while being aware of its toxicity.[20] The decision was considered by management and the board as rational and shareholder value–maximizing, on the ground that regulation was unenforced. As it turned out, regulators found out about the problem and inflicted a fine on the company, albeit a modest one, vindicating the management calculation. Eventually, the decision turned out to be disastrous to the environment, and also to shareholders (the company was ultimately forced to settle a $670 million class-action lawsuit), but not to the directors who rubber-stamped the decision. Overall, these examples highlight the fact that companies can remain within the boundaries of the law, comply with regulation or nearly so, yet inflict considerable damage on society. Even when there is a collective and nearly unanimous will to act (to regulate pollution, to regulate drugs, or to protect teenagers), the government can be far behind the curve. Regulating takes time and intense fights against lobbying efforts, and sometimes free-riding among nations prevents governments from acting, as they fear factories might move abroad.

Ambiguities of the Caring Corporation

In response to these concerns, the Business Roundtable, America's powerful lobby of large corporations, announced in 2019 a bold ambition to "redefine the purpose of the corporation": "While each of our individual companies serves its own corporate purpose, we share a fundamental commitment to *all* of our stakeholders. . . . Each of our stakeholders [customers, community, employees, suppliers, shareholders] is essential. We commit to deliver value to all of them, for the future success of our companies[,] our communities[,] and our country."[21] The big revolution in this statement is that top US managers support an equal weighting for shareholders, employees, customers, and other constituencies (environment, communities, and so on), a major deviation from the classic doctrine of shareholder primacy. Of course, nothing really happened. One year later, none of these companies had made any change to its corporate governance guidelines, except to reaffirm its commitment to shareholder value maximization.[22] This should come as no surprise: the talk of corporate social responsibility has been going on for a while but has never succeeded in changing the mandate of corporate managers.

For example, as early as 1932, the author of a *Harvard Law Review* article advocated for equal consideration by firms of shareholders, employees, and customers.[23] His stakeholderism was *not* instrumental, nor was it "merely a more intelligent appreciation of what tends to the ultimate benefit of stockholders." In his view, corporations were institutions too powerful to be run only in the interest of shareholders. They had a "social responsibility" to their employees (this article was written during the Great Depression). As a legal fix, the author proposed that corporate managers be trustees of companies themselves, as distinct institutions, rather than trustees of shareholders ("trustees for an institution rather than attorneys for the stockholders"). The author concluded the article by discussing the jurisprudence of the time that compelled companies more and more to recognize the "interests of other persons besides their owners." This jurisprudence, as we know now, failed to significantly change the mandate of corporate managers. They remained, until now, committed to shareholder value maximization.

If this is such an old idea, why hasn't it happened yet? The reason is that managers do not own the firm; they are mere "trustees" of the shareholder's investment in the firm. They would be in breach of their legal duties if they were to decide, on their own, to change the explicit objective of corporations. In the United States, the legal framework, since the early 1900s, binds trustees who manage other people's money to duties of care and loyalty to their beneficiaries, the shareholders (this is called the "fiduciary duty"). It is, of course, possible to change the objective of a firm and make it, say, more employee-friendly, but shareholders need to provide explicit consent, in a vote, since they are the rightful owners of the firm. Right after the Business Roundtable declaration, economist Luigi Zingales actually denounced the power grab of CEOs who have no mandate to deviate from shareholder wealth maximization.[24] But in the end, the coup did not even take place.

There are, however, cases where shareholders make the choice to weigh all stakeholders equally. In many US states, for instance, the statute of "Benefit Corporation" is available. Benefit Corporations can define mission statements that deviate from strict shareholder maximization. A famous example is the ice cream maker Ben & Jerry's, whose mission statement echoes the Business Roundtable's declaration: "In 1988, Ben & Jerry's was one of the first companies in the world to place a social mission in equal importance to its product and economic missions."[25] This happened because, at one point, the company's shareholders agreed to this, as did more recently the shareholders of Danone NA, Allbirds, or Patagonia.[26] Of course, this is easier to do when firms are created under this statute, because the founders embrace an idea of moral capitalism.

Thus, what prevents corporations from becoming more intrinsically moral entities is not the legal framework. But CEOs cannot make this decision for a company they do not own. They need to obtain the agreement of the company's stockholders, and until they do so, the only kind of altruism they can impose on companies is the instrumental one. This constraint exists for a good reason: broadening the objective is neither a blank check to managers nor a smokescreen behind which the incompetent can hide. CEOs of large, private corporations are selected to be assertive, confident, charismatic. These qualities are important to successfully run a firm, but they do not go well with a lack of accountability.

This discussion leaves us with a clear conclusion: the moral corporation is possible *if it does reflect the moral preferences of shareholders*. There is no reason why corporate owners would only care about money. Like everyone else, shareholders are altruistic human beings, and many of them would probably not condone outright immoral firm behavior (as our survey seems to suggest). It would therefore make sense to harness these prosocial proclivities of firm owners for the greater good and let them decide on the basis of these preferences. We would expect companies run by moral shareholders to weigh collective welfare at least a little bit and thus deviate from pure profit maximization. We will explore this specific issue of shareholder moral preferences in more detail in the next chapter.

Conclusion: The Fragmentation of Capitalism

To conclude this part of our discussion, let us highlight two challenges for the moral corporation. The first one, as we have seen above, is governance. Given the relative vagueness of its mission, making management accountable can be difficult. But it is not impossible. Many colleges, universities, hospitals, savings and loans, and Benefit Corporations have broader objectives than profit maximization yet manage to accomplish their missions while successfully competing with traditional, profit-oriented companies. The second challenge is the fragmentation of capitalism, as moral values are more diverse than ever, and politics are polarized. Firms may decide to source inputs from suppliers of their own country to avoid geopolitical dislocation. They may be unable to serve, at the same time, customers from different political leanings, as it may be perceived as duplicitous. They may be forced to take sides with regard to their employees on key issues such as gun control, reproductive rights, or gay rights. It is often hard for them to remain politically neutral, as demonstrated by the confrontation between Disney and the Republican governor of Florida.[27]

The difficulty of remaining politically neutral is well illustrated by the debate on reproductive rights in the United States. In the last few years, many US companies have started to offer their female employees options to get abortions out of state. This has happened because some states have started to impose various limitations on such procedures, a movement accelerated by the 2022 reversal of *Roe v. Wade* by the Supreme Court. Given how divided American politics are on this issue, these corporate decisions have been assimilated to political activism, by both pro-life and pro-choice groups. Such polarization is apparent in a question we asked our US participants:

> Some of the female employees of a large US firm are working in states where abortion is illegal. For employees who wish to get an abortion, the firm offers to pay for out of state travel and medical expenses.

For pregnant women who intend on giving birth, the firm would subsidize child care [half of the sample].

How much do you support this policy?

Reflecting nationwide support for women's reproductive rights, 56 percent of our respondents agree with the new company policy. But the political divide runs deep: 86 percent of the liberals and 20 percent of the conservatives. Conservative support increases by 2 percentage points if we add the statement that the firm will also subsidize child care. This controversy on reproductive rights led to a surge in shareholder scrutiny ahead of the 2023 general assembly meetings.[28] Overall, this example shows that firms have little scope for acting in a politically neutral manner on these issues (even if the motive is instrumental, not political). They are perceived as taking sides in the political debate.

Firms' controlling shareholders then have the choice between two options: remaining pluralistic (accommodate all values) or going tribal (pander to the tastes of specific sub-groups). Which force will dominate is of course impossible to tell, but it is clear that the days of the global, rootless, pan-cultural corporation are behind us—the world is no longer flat.

9
Money

Beyond just financial returns, our investment decisions have far-reaching consequences on the lives of others. As an example, imagine owning a farm that grows delicious fruits, but there's a catch: the land is secretly radioactive, which gives the fruits their exceptional taste. The problem is, this radiation poses a long-term health risk to consumers, even though nobody would suspect the connection between your products and their health issues. In this situation, it's clear that your moral responsibility is to stop producing these poisonous fruits, even if there are no rules forcing you to do so and even if nobody notices the harm you're causing.

Now, let's make things a little more complicated. You are no longer the manager but only the investor: you still own the piece of land that produces these toxic fruits but rent it out to a farmer. You've warned the farmer about the danger of the land for growing safe crops. As the landowner, do you have a responsibility to make sure the farmer doesn't sell toxic products? Things get a bit blurry. While you cannot be legally held accountable for the farmer's actions, can you really wash your hands of the problem? You could keep an eye on how the land is being used, and you could terminate the lease if you have doubts. However, if checking up on the farmer is costly or illegal, you might feel like you have no direct responsibility for how your land is being misused—you have done your part by informing the farmer. The chain of responsibility is less directly tied to you: It is his decision, not yours! And what if you chose to sell the land to another owner to avoid these moral complications: Is that a valid moral escape? If you warn the new owner about the land's dark secret before the transaction, it seems like a legitimate exit route. But is it really? Isn't there a risk that the buyer bought it *precisely because* they feel no moral constraint regarding growing and selling poisonous fruit? In fact, do you not have a moral obligation to ensure that the land is not exploited for agriculture?

This chapter is going to take us through the subtle debates on the moral responsibilities of corporate investors (people who finance companies, directly or indirectly, alone or with other investors), which this small example touches upon. The debates have both conceptual and practical dimensions. We will discuss various perspectives on what defines a moral investor.

Corporate Governance: Shareholders Have Control Rights

The ownership of the biggest companies is shared by a multitude of shareholders, who jointly own these companies. Their ownership of equity entitles them to collectively *control* what is done within those companies. For instance, if most shareholders disapprove of the strategy of a company, they can voice their discontent by voting against the decisions of management and even get the CEO removed. Alternatively, they can express their discontent by selling their shares to someone else, like the landowner in the example above. This way of expressing discontent is called "exit" (following the "exit v. voice" terminology coined by Albert Hirschman) or "voting with one's feet" (by analogy with a discontented citizen who would choose to move away or emigrate).[1] The mechanisms guaranteeing that shareholders can express their will by using their voting rights is called "corporate governance." Companies have corporate charters, which define the set of rules that allocate power within a company, in a manner analogous to that of the constitution for a nation. A critical function of corporate governance is to prevent the "entrenchment of managers," namely, a situation where managers would act as they like and potentially indulge in entertaining projects that are not profitable. Managers cannot be expected to spontaneously pass the baton to better executives when the situation so requires: governance is the mechanism that prevents the transformation of firms into CEO-ruled autocracies.

Corporate governance is mainly designed to make sure that businesses are run in a manner that serves and protects shareholders. But this also implies that company owners have a moral duty. They have a say on what the company does. The control rights coming with their shares constitute the lever that can drive change. If their company hurts others and they do not do anything about it, they cannot just wash their hands of it. By choosing to own or keep such companies, they are making a decision that carries moral weight.

The Moral Responsibility of Shareholders: An Old Idea

For the reasons mentioned above, thinking about the moral dimension of the act of investing is a natural idea. And it is also an old one. The roots of socially responsible investing are religious and are famously traced back to the Quakers. In 1758, the Quaker Philadelphia Yearly Meeting issued a decree barring its members from engaging in the slave trade, explicitly forbidding the buying or selling of human beings. John Wesley, the eighteenth-century theologian who cofounded the Methodist movement, encouraged people to carefully consider their moral responsibilities in economic matters. His teachings on money and investment, summarized in his famous sermon "The Use of Money," emphasized avoiding harm to one's neighbor through business practices and steering clear of industries such as tanning and chemical production, which potentially jeopardize workers' health.[2]

Following such principles, religious communities started excluding from their endowment portfolios the companies that, from their perspective, were not morally acceptable sources of profits. The first socially responsible mutual funds were launched by Pax World mutual fund family in August 1971. The founders, L. Tyson and J. Corbett, were United Methodist ministers and adamant to avoid investing their churches' assets in companies involved in the Vietnam War. The Pax World Fund thus excluded companies that manufactured war products such as napalm and Agent Orange—the latter an extremely powerful defoliant, sprayed by the army to expose enemy positions in the jungle, and which has been linked to a number of diseases. They then started to screen out tobacco companies, major polluters, and companies dealing in alcohol and gambling.

Over the following decade, South Africa, which practiced institutionalized racial segregation and discrimination (called apartheid) until 1994, was a defining topic for responsible investing. Several institutional investors, including university endowments, pension funds, and religious congregations, expressed their will to avoid investing in companies benefiting from activities in South Africa.[3] In 1986, California's state pension funds were divested from companies with activities in South Africa. US banks were under pressure from investors to stop making new loans in South Africa. For instance, Citicorp agreed to comply with this boycott, and in 1987 it sold its South African subsidiary.[4] This movement foreshadowed the Russian boycott discussed at the beginning of chapter 8.

Before we explore the practical aspects of responsible investing, it is crucial to explain certain challenges it faces. Modern capitalism presents two factors that tend to diminish shareholders' sense of responsibility.

Dispersed Shareholders, Diluted Responsibilities

First, there is the dispersion of control rights among myriad shareholders. Analogous to what happens to voters in democracies, this diffuses the sense of responsibility.

If a toxic person accesses power because too many citizens abstain from voting, it can be argued that each one of these abstainers bears some responsibility for the outcome of the election. However, in such situations, voters tend to justify their abstention by arguing that their lone vote wouldn't have been decisive. And they are right: one is indeed almost never individually pivotal in the result of an election. Dispersed responsibility diminishes our personal sense of duty. Every voter feels like just a whisper in a roaring crowd. This is not just speculation: empirical studies exploring moral decisions confirm this effect. Remember the experiment, briefly discussed in chapter 4, where participants had to decide on a disturbing moral question: Would they agree to kill (mice) for money?[5] The finding was that, in a group setting, participants were more likely to consent to this act, even if they would have refused individually: the collective dimension reduces moral discomfort.

Limited Liability: Another Challenge to Ethical Awareness

A second challenge in instilling a sense of responsibility in shareholders arises from a defining feature of modern capitalism: "limited liability." This legal status of modern companies ensures that when they face legal repercussions for societal damages, their owners are only liable up to the amount they invested in the company. Essentially, while a share price can plummet, it cannot venture into negative territory. At most, investors might lose their initial investment, but they will not be additionally liable for any harm the company might have caused beyond that.

Limited liability was generalized in the nineteenth century. It made it possible to harness the savings of the middle class for the financing of large, risky projects, such as railroad construction. In essence, the idea was to tell these savers: "There is upside in these projects, go for it. You should just be aware that some of these companies might get bankrupt, in which case you will lose your investment in them but no more."

The concept of limited liability is now commonplace, but its inception was met with apprehension over the potential erosion of moral responsibility. In essence, it not only dilutes moral responsibility but does much worse: it incentivizes financial risk-taking at society's expense. Consider an innovative project that, with a 50 percent chance, could generate $5 billion in economic value. But there is an equal chance it could result in $50 billion in societal loss, possibly due to health hazards. Under limited liability, shareholders might find investing in such a venture appealing: a significant gain on success and minimal loss on failure. If things take a turn for the worse, the company will simply declare bankruptcy, leaving victims with limited legal recourse. This happens even if courts rule ex-post that the company was not legally entitled to launch such a project, so regulation is not an easy fix. While victims could attempt to sue management under tort law, alleging intentional harm, such a route is challenging and uncertain: management might say, "We did not know at the time, we were just doing our job." Note that the more diversified shareholders are, the more such a gamble is attractive to them: after all, this is just one in thousands of companies they have in their portfolio. Still, morally, such a gamble is clearly unacceptable.

The infamous rise and fall of Purdue Pharma briefly mentioned in chapter 8 can serve as a stark illustration of this perverse mechanism. Controlled by the Sackler family, Purdue is widely criticized for having fueled the opioid epidemic through its prescription painkiller, OxyContin. The company caused immense social damage. The Sacklers have profited by billions from selling the addictive drug. Thanks to limited liability, they initially managed to protect a big part of their gains from legal claims by victims and their families through a settlement with eight US states approved by a bankruptcy court. Negotiated in the shadow of limited liability, this settlement was de facto putting a cap on the Sacklers' personal liability. The situation was so morally outrageous that in 2024, the US Supreme Court—to which the US trustee brought the matter—voided the deal. The Court decided, in a nutshell, that bankruptcy courts do not have the power to forgive this level of damage on behalf of society.[6]

The Rise of Responsible Investing: Antidote to Cold-Blooded Profit Maximization

Thus, the interplay between *diversification* and *limited liability* amplifies concerns that unchecked profit maximization could lead to socially harmful actions. This might be in the form of exploiting regulatory gaps (such as excessive risk-taking by banks) or making undue gambles to the detriment of society. However, the societal benefits of diversifying savings and enabling the middle class to access equity investments are significant. This underscores the importance of shareholders recognizing and embracing their moral responsibilities.

One can take solace in the fact that, despite the economic and legal forces that diminish their formal obligations, shareholders are increasingly sensitive to the theme of social responsibility. Maybe it is precisely because modern capitalism creates a crying need for its emergence as a counterweight to profit maximization that the shareholder responsibility movement has been getting traction.

Today, there are nearly four hundred sustainable mutual funds in the United States.[7] According to the US SIF Foundation, $7.6 trillion in US–domiciled assets, held by 497 institutional investors, can be considered as practicing responsible investing.[8] The rise of concerns over climate change and CO_2 emissions has empowered responsible investing, which has become mainstream. In fact, most large asset managers now have an "ESG" ("Environmental, Social, and Governance") department that screens companies, eliminates the most problematic ones, and sometimes engages portfolio companies to comply with objectives (such as CO_2 reduction targets) that go beyond the current legal constraints.

In a 2018 survey run on beneficiaries of a Dutch pension fund managing more than 20 billion euros, researchers found that two-thirds of the beneficiaries were supportive of the fund getting involved in socially responsible investing, even if they anticipated that this engagement might negatively impact financial results.[9] A primary driving factor behind this is participants' pronounced social inclinations. The idea of responsible investing is now largely mainstream.

Some Fuzziness on Financial Concessions

While the rise of responsible investing is something to celebrate, when we closely examine the marketing materials of responsible funds, we often encounter conceptual vagueness and even deliberate ambiguities that deserve to be highlighted.

First, regarding financial *performance*, very few funds are willing to admit any trade-off between profitability and moral responsibility. On the contrary, many claim that in the long run, the most responsible companies will yield the most spectacular stock performance for their investors. These funds are therefore framing the "win-win" paradigm discussed in the previous chapter, arguing that investors do not have to accept any compromise on their profits to express their moral preferences. They can be "smart" on both sides. The bet (sometimes implicitly made) here is that future regulations, particularly on climate, will become more restrictive and that the companies that are the most virtuous today will also be the most capable of integrating these new constraints. This is summarized by Joe Keefe, president of Impax Asset Management (a company that advises Pax World Funds):

> We believe that capital markets will be shaped profoundly by global sustainability challenges, particularly climate change, environmental pollution, natural resource constraints, and demographic and human capital issues such as diversity, inclusion, and equality. Our view is that these trends will drive growth for well-positioned companies and create risks for those unable or unwilling to adapt. We seek to invest in companies that are better prepared for the transition to a more sustainable economy and better at managing risk, including ESG-related risk. . . . Investing in companies that are better positioned for this transition is simply a smarter way to invest.[10]

This view is far from being absurd, but it requires a strong assumption, namely, that financial markets are inefficient and currently (irrationally) overvalue companies that do not take these trends into account (notice that climate change is lumped together with other issues, such as "resource constraints" or diversity). For instance, investors on Wall Street fail to understand that one day we will run out of copper. Or that carbon regulation will be more binding and that firms should anticipate this. Or that an inclusive HR policy will be needed to make profits. The stock price of firms that fail to anticipate the need to adapt is not lower, and the firms' managers keep their jobs even though they fail to anticipate those trends. That financial markets are so inefficient that prices do not incorporate future events like climate change is certainly possible, but it is a bit of a gamble, not something that should be presented as self-evident. After all, professional investors are paid to anticipate these risks, for instance, by selling stocks of mismanaged firms before their price collapses.

At a deeper level, the win-win argument in favor of responsible investing amounts to nullifying the moral question. It makes responsibility instrumental: if maximizing profits or avoiding certain risks requires considering extra-financial dimensions, such as carbon emissions, then yes, it is only natural that savvy investors would be concerned about these dimensions. Morality has nothing to do with the story: it is marketing icing on the cake of profit maximization. As we have said, morality becomes an important issue only when there is a real trade-off between profits and morality: you would have to be remarkably evil to choose to invest in "evil" unprofitable companies rather than "virtuous" profitable companies! When responsible funds deny the existence of this trade-off, they implicitly admit that they place little weight on ethical considerations.

What Are the Moral Objectives of Responsible Investing?

A second ambiguity of responsible investing is the vagueness of the moral objectives it tries to achieve. To simplify things, let us say that there are two primary ethical perspectives that seem to guide investors: *deontological ethics* and *consequentialism*. We already touched upon this dichotomy when we discussed altruism in chapter 2, but let us revisit these two types of moral preferences in the context of responsible investing.

Deontological ethics, which economists also call "value alignment," reflect investors' aversion to owning companies that do not align with their moral values. Concretely, such investors are averse to receiving profits from companies engaged in activities they deem morally objectionable. So, they do not want to own shares in such companies. The conceptual background behind such an approach is deontology, a view of ethical actions as complying with core principles, such as not profiting from activities that harm others, as argued by Reverend Wesley in his sermon about money. Derived from the Greek word *deon,* meaning "duty" or "what is right," deontology posits that certain actions are intrinsically right or wrong, irrespective of the consequences. As we explained in chapter 2, the renowned eighteenth-century German philosopher Immanuel Kant stands out as a leading proponent of this ethical approach. Kant posited that actions should comply with universal moral laws, grounded in reason, such as "Do not lie" and "Do not steal." In this duty-centered ethical viewpoint, the morality of actions is dictated not by their outcomes but by their inherent nature: the end never justifies the means.

In contrast, *consequentialism,* or impact-seeking behavior, is driven by the concern for the social consequences of investment decisions. Investors with consequentialist preferences value the social impact of their investment decisions. Avoiding "sinful" companies is not in itself an objective for such investors: what they want is to make a difference in the world. This ethical framework is particularly familiar to economists, who often employ cost-benefit analyses underpinned by utilitarian assumptions. In such analyses, the aggregate welfare resulting from a specific action, such as a particular investment decision, is compared to the scenario without that action. This comparison then informs whether the action is deemed beneficial or not.

As it turns out, this difference between *deontology* and *consequentialism* is crucial for the design of responsible savings products. Deontological investors avoid holding sinful companies and are therefore likely to be interested in investing in portfolios of firms with a good moral footprint (for example, companies with low carbon emissions, if one focuses on the environmental dimension). Such portfolios are not appealing to consequentialist investors: avoiding investment in "dirty companies" does not necessarily have a material impact on social welfare if these companies can finance their projects through other means. Conversely, buying companies that are already virtuous might not change the types of projects they undertake, or make them bigger. Consequentialist investors want to invest for *impact*. They are perfectly fine subsidizing green investments (understand: accept lower returns) to chase brown investments from the market. They may prefer to encourage a brown firm to reform itself than to invest in an already green company. Overall, they do not just want to buy a portfolio of well-behaved companies. They prefer a fund that tips the balance even if that means lower returns.

Companies' Impact vs. Investors' Impact

A common mistake is to confuse the impact of a company's business decisions and the impact of investors buying into that company's stock. For instance, if Joseph buys stocks in a company that is installing solar panels (so the firm has impact on the world), he is not really helping climate change mitigation (he has no impact on the company). Let us explain how this works. When Joseph buys stocks, he buys them from a *seller*. His cash does not go to the company, nor is it used to produce more green energy: it goes to the seller's bank account. Now, in some rare instances, when companies try to grow, they sell new stocks for cash (which is called *equity issuances*). The buyers of stocks do, in this case, transfer money to the firm. If Joseph participates in such a sale of new stocks, he only really helps if he pays *more* than the other, purely profit-driven, buyers. This cannot happen, however, because Joseph is not the only buyer. The company needs to convince the other buyers and therefore sell its new shares at the (lower) price they are willing to accept. This is the tragedy of responsible investing: unless Joseph and people like him buy *all* the stocks, the price will be set by morally agnostic investors, and he cannot subsidize the firm. The bottom line is this: if some investors are willing to act as purely profit-driven investors, the "boycotts" by a few deontological investors cannot be expected to have a significant impact.

At this stage, you may recall your high school economics training and wonder: Why doesn't the law of supply and demand work here? Even if there are few deontological investors like Joseph, one would still expect that they increase the demand for green stock a little, which would raise the stock price of the solar panel installer by a small amount. This would encourage the company to sell new stocks and finance new projects. What is wrong here? In all fairness, this common-sense reasoning is correct, but this effect is so small that it is likely to be negligible. Economists Jonathan Berk and Jules Van Binsbergen estimate it to be of the order of 0.004 percent: by shunning brown stocks, green investors decrease their value by 0.4 *basis points*.[11] Their impact is tiny because, for all the fuss made by the financial industry around green investment, there are not that many green investors (about 10 percent of the US mutual funds).[12] As soon as one of the brown stocks they boycott drops in value (relative to its future profits), the 90 percent of other investors are happy to substitute a few of their green stocks for this brown stock, and this plays the role of a powerful shock absorber for the price of this brown stock. Note that this is different from the logic of consumer boycotts: for instance, if European consumers boycott a given car company because it has lied on its environmental impact, it will sell fewer cars and make less profit. Now, if European shareholders collectively refuse to hold shares of that company, they will sell these shares, and the stocks will just be held by other investors: the total number of shares does not shrink, contrary to the number of cars produced in case of a consumer boycott. This is why virtuous investors cannot expect to have as much impact as virtuous consumers. Consumer boycott is simply more effective than shareholder boycott.

The Unwanted Effects of Shareholder Boycotts

In fact, there is an even more "perverse effect" of shareholder boycotts: if polluting companies perceive that moral investors are rejecting them, they might just give up on improving themselves. Economists Sam Hartzmark and Kelly Shue discuss several reasons why ESG investing is discouraging. For instance, "green investors" celebrate firms that manage to reduce their emissions by a large *percentage*. But this type of "proportional thinking" is toxic to global emissions. It leads investors to reward the reduction of one ton of CO_2 about 260 times more if it comes from an already green firm than if it comes from a brown firm.[13] This is, of course, highly inefficient, since reducing emissions by one ton has the same effect on climate whether this reduction comes from a brown or a green firm.

Another unwanted consequence of the deontological approach in terms of its impact is that it encourages large companies that want to appeal to deontological investors to sell their dirty assets to other, less responsible investors. This has happened to many of the coal plants previously owned by well-known energy companies. Over the last two decades, some of these plants have been sold to private equity funds that are not accountable to deontological investors, and these plants are still active today: the planet is not better off.

Impact Investing: Shareholder Activism or Private Markets

In contrast, impact investors approach their investments with a different perspective. Avoiding sin stocks is not an objective per se for them. Their primary concern is the tangible difference their investment can make. Thus, they tend to favor funds that actively engage with the management of companies that have room for improvement, with the aim of persuading them to implement these enhancements. This could involve opting for less polluting production technologies, for instance. Following this logic, impact investors do not necessarily avoid investing in companies with less-than-stellar ethical records, provided they believe they can influence these (this is a form of shareholder activism). Going back to the logic of Hartzmark and Shue, it is much easier to squeeze a given amount of CO_2 emission reduction from a brown firm than from an already green firm.

Alternatively, impact investors may choose to finance firms that are capital constrained but have a positive impact on the world. They target firms with high social value projects but insufficient financial value to attract traditional capital. This is why some impact funds specifically target projects that would not receive financing without their intervention. As much as possible, these funds strive to document the "additionality" of their investment, which refers to the specific difference their investment strategy makes. Such funds typically invest not in companies traded on the stock market but rather in smaller businesses, so that they can have more impact on the existence and the scale of these projects. For example, an impact venture capital fund can focus on financing startups that find solutions for carbon capture but are financially constrained because these projects are very uncertain.

Consequentialism or Deontology: An Experiment

In a real-world experiment involving actual participants and real money, we have sought (with Pari Sastry and Jean-François Bonnefon) to determine whether people lean more toward consequentialism or deontology when it comes to responsible investing.[14] To achieve this, we did the following: we auctioned several types of hypothetical company shares to participants. All these stocks were paying cash dividends to their owner. On top of this, some companies were virtuous (donating a portion of profits to charities), while others were toxic (reducing donations that we, the experimenters, had pledged to charities). Note that while the companies were fictitious, the money was not. For instance, a stock would promise to pay a dividend of 50 cents and give a donation of 20 cents to Save the Children. The participant would then be asked to bid for the stock and would cash in the difference between 50 cents and the purchase price.

We found that participants, for a given level of cash dividend, were willing to pay more for virtuous companies. Another surprising finding was that participants did not seem to care whether their act of purchasing influenced the ethical behavior of the companies or not, suggesting a full-on deontologist moral orientation. How did we show this? Two different groups of participants were exposed to slightly different versions of the experiment. In the first group, the hypothetical companies made their donations (or confiscations) *regardless* of the participant's ownership. In the second group, these charity transfers occurred *only if* the buyer's bid was high enough. If participants were consequentialists, they should not be willing to pay more than the purely financial value of the stock in the first case but should be willing to pay more for a charitable company in the second case, as a high enough bid actually *causes* the donation. However, we found no difference at all between these two treatments.

There was another surprise. Some participants were allowed to donate part of their earnings to the charity directly, but they would almost never do it. Think about it: they were willing to pay more for a firm that was donating to a charity, even though this firm would be donating anyway. However, they avoided donating money directly to the charity. A true consequentialist would pay the minimum price for the virtuous firm and use the saved amount to donate directly. But our deontological investors preferred to give extra money to the *seller* of the stock (that is, us, the experimenters) than to the charity.

Did participants truly understand what was happening, or were they confused? It turns out that this behavior was not due to a lack of understanding. The experiment verifies through a quiz that participants understood whether their actions were consequential or not. Investors' valuations of corporate donations were highly significant, regardless of whether their purchase decision caused the donations or not. This suggests that in this setting, value alignment largely dominated, and impact concerns were negligible.

Deontology Is Not Irrational

Economists, who are mostly trained as consequentialists, might be tempted to say that deontologists are just irrational or, to use a euphemism from behavioral economics, that their rationality is "bounded" (by their cognitive limitations). But this assessment is both unfair and borderline paternalistic. After all, it is perfectly coherent to be concerned about whether our wealth sources align with our values. And this is not only philosophically backed, it seems highly prevalent in common-sense moral thinking. There are various situations that make clear that a consequentialist approach will not do, and most of us expect some form of deontological behavior. Take, for instance, the case of donations from a dubious source. Foundations or universities that take money from corporate villains, criminals, or oppressive regimes that do not respect human rights are deeply embarrassed later when this is revealed to the public. Why is that? After all, a pure consequentialist approach would say that it is not the origin of money that counts but only its use (let us assume here that the nonprofits in question are indeed contributing to the common good). Still, it seems intuitively morally appalling. It may reflect a lack of integrity on the part of the nonprofit ("If they take dirty money, how can they be honest in their other dealings?"). It may also be perceived as a form of moral complacency contributing to trivializing bad behavior ("By taking money from a repressive regime, they are making human rights violations more acceptable.").

Let us dig a bit on why being principle-oriented as the deontologists are is not more irrational than being consequentialist. The two philosophies are in fact not so much in contradiction with each other as they seem. As we said in chapter 2, the Kantian reasoning is that *if everyone was behaving like this,* the world would be a better place. It applies to responsible investing, since in this case, "sin" companies would de facto be deprived of capital (their stock price would drop to zero). The fact that there are some amoral or immoral investors willing to substitute does not delegitimize this desire for ethical coherence.

Reconciling Deontology and Consequentialism

In fact, the distinction between deontology and consequentialism is less airtight than it looks. One way to reconcile the two traditions is called rule-consequentialism. The idea is as follows: to avoid making mistakes, being caught by time, or even deceiving ourselves when faced with moral choices, it is more reliable to adopt a certain number of simple rules. These rules can be chosen because their consequences are desirable, that is, they are optimal from a consequentialist point of view. Of course, these rules may lack flexibility and may fail to generate the best outcome in each specific context. But they have, on average, the right consequences. For instance, "do not lie" may be the right ethical rule to follow in general (because lying is using other people and therefore negating their autonomy), but there may be specific situations in which it will have bad consequences (such as when saving a friend's life demands that we lie to the gangsters who are looking for him). These situations happen so rarely that the rule "do not lie" is the right one from a rule-consequentialist viewpoint. Another big advantage of rules is that they protect us from the temptation to not do what is right. An "end justifies the means" mindset is dangerous, as giving ourselves the flexibility to optimize as a function of the context might lead us to decisions that afterward appear foolish because there was a risk that we did not foresee. Sticking to rules can be more robust to our temptations or our cognitive mistakes.

Another approach to reconcile deontology and consequentialism is to consider that there is a form of exemplarity in the deontological attitude: we hope that, in the long run, our attitude will be generalized, as others will be convinced to follow our example. We may even want to set an example for our future selves and stay away from the slippery slope of moral drift. This bet on the "contagion" of moral actions is also akin to a consequentialist approach.

Climate Change: A Case Study

Climate change is a natural application ground for responsible investing. It is also a good example to recap some of the ideas we have seen.

First, why doesn't regulation tackle the issue? There is widespread international consensus that CO_2 emissions are too high and that mechanisms such as carbon taxes or markets for emission permits are needed to encourage firms to innovate. There are several reasons why this is not happening at a satisfactory scale. The first problem is international free-riding: governments worry that if they impose strict regulations while other countries do not, businesses might pack up and leave for more cost-effective locations. Second, politicians tend to have short-term incentives; they must win reelection and cannot afford to slow down the economy. And for that same reason, they cannot commit to implementing tougher regulations in the future: most of them will not even be in power in four or five years.

So, this underreaction of governments leaves room for responsible investors to step in to try to influence companies. As we have discussed, one option consists of engaging with companies and demanding that they make their production greener (for instance, by asking oil companies to transition to renewables or IT firms to invest in less heat-generating servers). But, in practice, most of the responsible investing is passive. It consists of banks redirecting lending to greener industries and stockholders switching polluting companies' stocks for those of more environment-friendly companies. We have seen that this is a respectable goal but with limited impact. As we said previously, it may even be counterproductive, because firms cater to deontological investors by selling their CO_2-producing assets to financiers that are unconcerned with climate issues. This has the effect of sweeping the problems under the carpet.

This deluge of passive, deontological funds in climate-related projects may raise concerns. Could responsible finance be a deceptive distraction, leading the public to believe that the private sector alone can tackle climate change? If the public starts to believe the financial industry has climate change under control, this could postpone vital government regulations. This is the thesis of Tariq Fancy, a whistleblower who once headed sustainable investing at BlackRock, the world's largest asset manager. He loudly exited the firm in 2021, harshly criticizing the asset management industry for comforting investors with feel-good greenwashing: "Most of what we were doing wasn't really creating any systemic change as much as lulling a fantasy that was delaying the action by government required to create that."[15]

We stand behind some of Tariq Fancy's critiques: the asset management sector must cease its climate marketing charades. It needs to present more objectively the actual impact of its actions. Yet, does responsible investing really discourage government intervention? We could argue the opposite. By creating a critical mass of companies that try to reduce their emissions, responsible investors finance innovations that can spill over to the rest of the economy, making it cheaper for everyone to reduce emissions. A virtuous circle kicks in: because firms will more easily adopt greener technology, government regulation can become more stringent (it will not hurt firms too much). Expecting such regulation will in turn encourage firms to innovate more today.[16] In this light, responsible investing and governmental actions can be seen as complementary forces, rather than as substitutes. A critical mass of deontological investors may be enough to have a real impact.

Conclusion

As the saying goes, "the road to hell is paved with good intentions." Simply having good intentions not only may fail to resolve complex issues but could inadvertently make matters worse. For this reason, it is imperative for investment funds focusing on responsible investment to be explicit about their objectives. This goes beyond mere feel-good marketing. It involves the critical differentiation between deontological motives and those driven by actual social or environmental impact. Equally vital is communicating to the public that simply avoiding certain stocks may not be the silver bullet for solving climate change.

Afterword

This book was inspired by a certain discomfort that we have felt as economists. We as a profession aim to promote the "common good," but we often rely on a simplistic notion of it (maximize efficiency, the sum of materialistic well-beings of people). This notion does not do justice to the diversity of moral viewpoints. It will seem obvious to most readers, especially at the end of this book, but the true "common good" is not a simple, unique, obvious objective. It is a construct that can only emerge from deliberation among citizens, from complex layers of moral considerations.

Conversely, in morally loaded public debates, economists are often right to point out that moral emotions are expressed without much appreciation of economic forces. Our instinct cries that the cold economic calculus does not have a place in our moral predicaments, that ethics are the domain of "whatever it takes," where economics simply does not belong. We do not think this view is correct either: economics is often part of the dilemma and cannot be ignored.

Though it is a tempting route, separating the economy from ethics is thus not an option. This book is an attempt both to bring economics to moral debates and conversely to bring moral pluralism to economic affairs. As others have said before us, economics is not a "morally free zone,"[1] but all the same, morality rarely is an "economics free zone." We are hoping to build this two-way street between our material interests and our ethical aspirations.

But then, how should we proceed? What is the method we recommend when difficult decisions arise? Unlike most economists, we do not offer a calculus (maximizing efficiency while avoiding inequalities) that can be blindly trusted to spit out the right answer. The main message of our book is a call for pluralism: it emphasizes the need to understand and incorporate diverse perspectives on moral-economic trade-offs. This pluralistic approach acknowledges that different persons may prioritize different, yet equally legitimate, values, such as freedom, justice, tradition, or economic efficiency. Some trade-offs are simple enough that the standard cost-benefit analysis can be used (they are purely "economic"). But this is not the case with "big decisions," such as immigration policy, inheritance taxes, cultural policy, globalization, and so forth. The complex layers of moral viewpoints cannot in such cases be summarized by a single welfare objective that individuals or policymakers should aim to maximize.

To make progress, the notion of "agreeing to disagree" is, in our view, the important first step. Recognizing various moral perspectives on economic issues facilitates discussions about difficult choices. In a conversation, each party brings forward their reasons and tries to convince others. "Agreeing to disagree" is a necessary condition to maintain peace and respect among differing viewpoints and to foster deliberation.

Economists should participate in this deliberation by exploring, more systematically than they currently are, the different value implications of economic policies—not just implications for inequality but also implications for freedom, justice, identity, tradition, or communities. Surveys, as we have demonstrated throughout the book, can help do that. How to weight these different values is, however, not up to economists. This is the role of politicians, community organizers, citizens, all of us.

Of course, even the most informed, serene, and polite conversations do not end up with everyone agreeing. It would be an illusion to hope that deliberation can lead to the convergence of viewpoints. Yet, ultimately, collective choices sometimes need to be made. This part is left by our book as an open question: How do societies reach final decisions amid inevitable disagreements from diverse values? How can we best aggregate different wills and reasons? How can we manage decisions that are unpopular to many citizens? These interrogations set the stage for another intellectual and practical project.

Notes

Preface

1. Michael Specter, "The Dangerous Philosopher," *New Yorker*, August 29, 1999.
2. D. J. Chalmers, "Why Isn't There More Progress in Philosophy?," *Philosophy* 90, no. 1 (2015): 3–31.
3. Michael Sandel, *What Money Can't Buy: The Moral Limits of Markets* (Penguin Books, 2012).
4. Angus Deaton, "Rethinking My Economics," *IMF Finance and Development* (2024).
5. See, for instance, the research of Paola Sapienza and Luigi Zingales, "Economists vs. Average Americans," *AEA Papers and Proceedings* (2013).

Chapter One

1. Rebecca Robbins and Stephanie Nolen, "A Dilemma for Governments: How to Pay for Million-Dollar Therapies?," *New York Times*, January 24, 2023.
2. Daniel Kahneman, *Thinking, Fast and Slow* (Farrar, Straus & Giroux, 2011).
3. Paul Tetlock, "Thinking the Unthinkable: Sacred Values and Taboo Cognitions," *Trends in Cognitive Sciences* (2003).
4. Michael Sandel, *What Money Can't Buy: The Moral Limits of Markets* (Harvard University Press, 2012).
5. Adam Smith, *An Inquiry into the Nature and Causes of the Wealth of Nations* (University of Chicago Press, 1977).
6. See on this subject the summary by Paul Seabright, Jonathan Stieglitz, and Karine Van der Straeten, "Evaluating Social Contract Theory in Light of Evolutionary Social Science," *Evolutionary Human Sciences* (2021).
7. Albert O. Hirschman, *The Passions and the Interests: Political Arguments for Capitalism before Its Triumph* (Princeton University Press, 2013).
8. Hirschman draws this idea from Montesquieu's statement that "it is fortunate for men to be in a situation where, though their passions may prompt them to be wicked, they have nevertheless an interest in not being so." Keynes also shared this view, but

expressed it in a more provocative way: in essence, he said that there are few passions more innocent than the desire to make money.

9. Deirdre McCloskey, "Bourgeois Virtue and the History of P and S," *Journal of Economic History* 58, no. 2 (1998): 297–317.
10. Jeremy Bentham, *An Introduction to the Principles of Morals and Legislation*, in *The Collected Works of Jeremy Bentham* (Oxford University Press, 1998).
11. Jon Elster, "Emotions and Economic Theory," *Journal of Economic Literature* 36, no. 1 (1998): 47–74.
12. This example is a paraphrase of the philosopher Robert Nozick's "experience machine." See, for instance, the "experience machine" Wikipedia entry, https://en.wikipedia.org/wiki/Experience_machine.
13. Robert Wiblin and Keilan Harris, "Economist Tyler Cowen Says Our Overwhelming Priorities Should Be Maximizing Economic Growth and Making Civilization More Stable. Is He Right?," *80000 Hours*, podcast (2018).
14. Jonathan Haidt, *The Righteous Mind: Why Good People Are Divided by Politics and Religion* (Random House, 2012).
15. William MacAskill, *Doing Good Better: Effective Altruism and a Radical New Way to Make a Difference* (Guardian Books, 2015).
16. David Bourget and David Chalmers, "What Do Philosophers Believe?," *Philosophical Studies: An International Journal for Philosophy in the Analytic Tradition* (2014).
17. Gary Becker and George Stigler, "De Gustibus Non Est Disputandum," *American Economic Review* (1977).
18. Augustin Landier, Parinitha Sastry, David Sraer, and David Thesmar, "Moral Tradeoffs in the COVID Crisis," unpublished paper (2020).

Chapter Two

1. Peter Singer, "Famine, Affluence and Morality," *Philosophy and Public Affairs* (1972).
2. William MacAskill, *Doing Good Better: Effective Altruism and a Radical New Way to Make a Difference* (Guardian Books, 2015).
3. This question is borrowed from the Moral Foundations Questionnaire, a classic series of questions written by a group of moral psychologists. The questionnaire can be found at https://moralfoundations.org/questionnaires/. The website also cites publications that contributed to develop the questionnaire or used it.
4. Jim A. C. Everett et al., "Moral Dilemmas and Trust in Leaders during a Global Health Crisis," *Nature Human Behaviour* 5, no. 8 (2021): 1074–88.
5. Cited in Amartya Sen, "Rational Fools: A Critique of the Behavioral Foundations of Economic Theory," *Philosophy and Public Affairs* (1977).
6. Sen, "Rational Fools."
7. Émile Durkheim, *The Division of Labor in Society* (Free Press, 2014).
8. Émile Durkheim, *Sciences sociales et action* (Presses Universitaires de France, 1970).
9. The story of this rift, from Auguste Comte to Bourdieu through Durkheim, is remarkably explained by Philippe Steiner in his book *Donner . . . Une histoire de l'altruisme* (Presses Universitaires de France, 2016).
10. Sen, "Rational Fools."
11. Adam Smith, *The Theory of Moral Sentiments*, ed. K. Haakonssen (Cambridge University Press, 2002), part 1, sec. 1, chap. 1, par. 3.
12. For a more comprehensive coverage of this literature, see James Andreoni, William Harbaugh, and Lise Westerlund, "Altruism in Experiments," in *New Palgrave Dictionary in Economics* (Macmillan, 2007).

13. Amory Gethin, Clara Martinez-Toledano, and Thomas Piketty, "Brahmin Left Versus Merchant Right: Changing Political Cleavages in 21 Western Democracies: 1948–2020," *Quarterly Journal of Economics* (2022).
14. See Benjamin Enke, Matthias Polborn, and Alex Wu, "Values as Luxury Goods and Political Polarization," NBER working paper 30001 (2022). For a review, see also Moses Shayo and Alon Harel, "Non-Consequentialist Voting," *Journal of Economic Behavior and Organizations* (2012).
15. This literature is too large to cite exhaustively. See, for example, on family businesses, M. Bennedsen, K. Meisner Nielsen, F. Perez-Gonzalez, and D. Wolfenzohn, "Inside the Family Firms: The Role of Families in Succession Decisions and Performance," *Quarterly Journal of Economics* (2007). On the subject of corporate board connections, one can read F. Kramarz and D. Thesmar, "Social Networks in the Boardroom," *Journal of the European Economic Association* (2012); and M. Bertrand, F. Kramarz, A. Schoar, and D. Thesmar, "The Cost of Political Connections," *Review of Finance* 22, no. 3 (2018): 849–76. On favoritism in government, see Guo Xu, "The Cost of Patronage: Evidence from the British Empire," *American Economic Review* (2018).
16. Montesquieu, *My Thoughts*, trans. and ed. Henry C. Clark (Liberty Fund, 2012).
17. Adam Smith, *The Theory of Moral Sentiments* (Penguin Classics, 2010).
18. Ben Enke, Ricardo Rodriguez-Padilla, and Florian Zimmermann, "Moral Universalism: Measurement and Economic Relevance," *Management Science* 68, no. 5 (2022): 3590–603.
19. Michael Sandel, *Justice: What's the Right Thing to Do?* (Macmillan, 2009).
20. Kwame Anthony Appiah, *Ethics of Identity* (Princeton University Press, 2005).
21. For an overview of his thinking, see, for example, Robert Putnam, "*E Pluribus Unum*: Diversity and Community in the Twenty-First Century—The 2006 Johan Skytte Prize Lecture," *Scandinavian Political Studies* (2007).
22. Anne Case and Angus Deaton, *Deaths of Despair and the Future of Capitalism* (Princeton University Press, 2020). Putnam's latest book, *The Upswing*, published in 2019, makes the connection with Durkheim's observation. The thesis of this book is that the level of individualism is returning, in the 2000s, to its nineteenth-century level.
23. The original article is James Andreoni, "Impure Altruism and Donations to Public Goods: A Theory of Warm-Glow Giving," *Economic Journal* 100, no. 401 (1990): 464–77.
24. For a recent paper on this, see Mark Ottoni-Wilhelm, Lise Vesterlund, and Huan Xie, "Why Do People Give? Testing Pure and Impure Altruism," *American Economic Review* (2017).
25. Immanuel Kant, *Groundwork of the Metaphysics of Morals*, trans. Mary Gregor (1785; Cambridge University Press, 1997), 15 (Akademie pagination 4:402).
26. Eddy Awad, Azim Sohan Dsouza, and Jean-François Bonnefon, "Universals and Variations in Moral Decisions Made in 42 Countries and 70,000 Participants," *Proceedings of the National Academy of Sciences* (2020). One limitation of studies based on variants of the trolley problem is the focus on "life or death" situations, which make consequentialists look like dangerous sociopaths. Work from the psychologist Guy Kahane shows that trolley problems test for the presence of two separate psychological traits: "impartiality" and "acceptance of instrumental harm." People who accept to sacrifice one life to save five are people who (1) are more impartial (one life is one life, whether you die in the "status quo" or as a result on my action) and (2) more tolerant to sacrificial harm (killing is justified if it saves lives). See Guy Kahane et al., "Beyond Sacrificial Harm: A Two-Dimensional Model of Utilitarian Psychology," *Psychological Review* (2017).
27. Roland Bénabou, Armin Falk, and Luca Henkel, "Ends versus Means: Kantians, Utilitarians and Moral Decisions," working paper (2022).

28. See, e.g., Carol Gilligan, *In a Different Voice: Psychological Theory and Women's Development* (Harvard University Press, 1982).
29. J. J. C. Smart and Bernard Williams, *Utilitarianism, For or Against* (Cambridge University Press, 1973).
30. Samuel Sigal, "Effective Altruism Gave Rise to Sam Bankman-Fried. Now It's Facing a Moral Reckoning," *Vox* (2022).
31. David Brooks, "The Way to Produce a Person," *New York Times*, 2022.

Chapter Three

1. Ronan Farrow and Jia Tolentino, "Britney's Conservatorship Nightmare," *New Yorker*, 2021.
2. Isaiah Berlin, "Two Concepts of Liberty," in *Four Essays on Liberty* (Oxford University Press, 1969).
3. Rousseau, *The Social Contract and Other Later Political Writings*, ed. and trans. Victor Gourevitch (1762; Cambridge University Press, 1997).
4. Paul Seabright, Jonathan Stieglitz, and Karine Van der Straeten, "Evaluating Social Contract Theory in Light of Evolutionary Social Science," *Evolutionary Human Sciences* (2021).
5. Berlin, "Two Concepts of Liberty."
6. Isaiah Berlin, *The Hedgehog and the Fox* (Princeton University Press, 1953).
7. See discussion on this in George Crowder, "Two Concepts of Liberal Pluralism," *Political Theory* (2007).
8. Joseph Schumpeter, *Capitalism, Socialism and Democracy* (Payot, 1951; originally published 1942).
9. The famous reference here is Friedrich von Hayek, "The Use of Knowledge in Society," *American Economic Review* (1945).
10. Paul A. Samuelson and William D. Nordhaus, *Economics*, 13th ed. (McGraw-Hill, 1989).
11. J. R. Hicks, *Wealth and Welfare* (Blackwell, 1981), 138.
12. Victor Hugo, *Les Misérables*, trans. Lee Fahnestock and Norman MacAfee (Signet Classics, 2013).
13. In particular, as Assar Lindbeck notes, this would allow a revisiting of competition issues: being able to buy from different suppliers is a freedom whose value exists beyond questions of price and quality of the products I buy. See Assar Lindbeck, "Individual Freedom and Welfare State Policy," *European Economic Review* (1988).
14. See Phillip P. Marzluf, "Literacy under Authority: The Mongolian Cultural Campaigns," *Journal of Asian Studies* 76, no. 1 (2017): 135–57.
15. This is a very active research topic for which the consensus is still emerging: overall, the social sciences suggest a reality that is far more subtle than the simplistic sounding-board theory. See Gordon Pennycook and David Rand, "The Psychology of Fake News," *Trends in Cognitive Sciences* (2021), for a summary of the literature. See also Seth Flaxman, Sharad Goel, and Justin M. Rao, "Filter Bubbles, Echo Chambers, and Online News Consumption," *Public Opinion Quarterly* 80, no. S1 (2016): 298–320; Matthew Gentzkow and Jesse M. Shapiro, "Ideological Segregation Online and Offline," *Quarterly Journal of Economics* 126, no. 4 (November 2011).
16. Economists Charles Angelucci and Andrea Prat review the large literature on public opinion. They also show that on a panel of important news items, people's beliefs are essentially correct: the percentage of those who believe a piece of news to be true and a piece of news to be false is quite low, and this is true for both Democrats

and Republicans. Charles Angelucci and Andrea Prat, "Is Journalistic Truth Dead? Measuring How Informed Voters Are about Political News," SSRN working paper (2020).

17. A. M. Guess, N. Malhotra, J. Pan et al., "How Do Social Media Feed Algorithms Affect Attitudes and Behavior in an Election Campaign?," *Science* 381, no. 6656 (2023): 398–404. See also Jeff Tollefson, "Tweaking Facebook Feeds Is No Easy Fix for Polarization, Studies Find," *Nature*, July 27, 2023, https://www.nature.com/articles/d41586-023-02420-z, for a summary of these studies.
18. Arlie Russell Hochschild, *Strangers in Their Own Land: Anger and Mourning on the American Right* (New Press, 2016).
19. Dean Karlan, Aishwarya Lakshmi Ratan, and Jonathan Zinman, "Savings By and For the Poor: A Research Review and Agenda," *Review of Income and Wealth* 60, no. 1 (2014): 36–78.
20. Richard H. Thaler and Cass R. Sunstein, *Nudge: Improving Decisions about Health, Wealth, and Happiness* (Yale University Press, 2008).
21. Andrew Gelman, "Nudgelords: Given Their Past Track Record, Why Should I Trust Them This Time? (Don't Call Me Stasi)," Twitter post, February 7, 2021.

Chapter Four

1. John Maynard Keynes, *The General Theory of Employment, Interest and Money* (Macmillan, 1936), chap. 24.
2. Joseph R. Biden, "Remarks by President Biden at Signing of an Executive Order Promoting Competition in the American Economy," The White House, July 9, 2021, State Dining Room, Washington, DC.
3. Émile Durkheim, *The Division of Labor in Society*, trans. W. D Halls (Free Press, 2014).
4. Durkheim, *The Division of Labor in Society.*
5. Max Weber, *The Protestant Ethic and the Spirit of Capitalism* (Routledge, 2005).
6. Durkheim, *The Division of Labor in Society.*
7. Paul Brook, "The Alienated Heart: Hochschild's Emotional Labour Thesis and the Anticapitalist Politics of Alienation," *Capital and Class* 33, no. 2 (2009): 7–31.
8. Arlie Russell Hochschild, "The Outsourced Self," *New York Times*, 2012.
9. A. Falk, T. Neuber, and N. Szech, "Diffusion of Being Pivotal and Immoral Outcomes," *Review of Economic Studies* (2020).
10. U. Gneezy and A. Rustichini, "Pay Enough or Don't Pay At All," *Quarterly Journal of Economics* 115, no. 3 (2000): 791–810.
11. Raghuram Rajan, *The Third Pillar: How Markets and the State Leave the Community Behind* (Penguin, 2019).
12. This intuition is found many times over in the economic literature. It is pedagogically expressed in Andrei Shleifer and Lawrence H. Summers, "Breach of Trust in Hostile Takeovers," *Corporate Takeovers: Causes and Consequences* (University of Chicago Press, 1988). The Nobel Prize–winning economist Oliver Hart has argued in several settings that a solution to this problem is ownership: in our discussion, employees would need to own the firm to prevent it from opportunistically reneging.
13. Eli Berman, "Sect, Subsidy and Sacrifice: An Economist's View of Ultra-Orthodox Jews," *Quarterly Journal of Economics* (2000).
14. This tension is well illustrated in the TV show *Unorthodox*, which features a young Hasidic woman, who is forced into an arranged marriage, and ultimately breaks free from her community. The Hasidic community is portrayed as oppressive, but at the

same time warm and full of humanity, with deeply felt religious ceremonies and joyful gatherings.

15. Henrik Cronqvist, Mitch Warachka, and Frank Yu, "Does Finance Make Us Less Social?," University of Miami Business School Research Paper 3229344 (2021).
16. G. Agneman and E. Chevrot-Bianco, "Market Participation and Moral Decision-Making: Experimental Evidence from Greenland," *Economic Journal* 133, no. 650 (2023): 537–81.
17. Marianne Bertrand and Francis Kramarz, "Does Entry Regulation Hinder Job Creation? Evidence from France," *Quarterly Journal of Economics* 117, no. 4 (2002): 1369–1413.
18. Yann Algan, Clément Malgouyres and Claudia Sénik, "Territories, Well-Being and Public Policy," *Notes du CAE* 55 (January 2020).
19. Elizabeth Popp Berman, *Thinking Like an Economist: How Efficiency Replaced Equality in U.S. Public Policy* (Princeton University Press, 2022).
20. Popp Berman, *Thinking Like an Economist*, ties this shift to the rising influence of the Chicago school. Filippo Lancieri, Eric A. Posner, and Luigi Zingales ("The Political Economy of the Decline of Antitrust Enforcement in the United States," BFI working paper [2022]) relate this to active lobbying of the US Chamber of Commerce and decision made by unelected judges.
21. J. Graham, B. A. Nosek, J. Haidt, R. Iyer, S. Koleva, and P. H. Ditto, "Mapping the Moral Domain," *Journal of Personality and Social Psychology* 101, no. 2 (2011): 366–85.
22. Participants are asked to indicate their level of agreement (on a scale from 1 to 5) with each one of the following four questions: (1) "I think it is morally wrong that rich children inherit a lot of money while poor children inherit nothing" (fairness); (2) "Compassion for those who suffer is the most crucial moral value" (compassion); (3) "People should be loyal to their family members, even when they have done something wrong" (loyalty); and (4) "Respect for authority is something children need to learn" (authority).
23. Augustin Landier and David Thesmar, "Who Is Neoliberal? Durkheimian Individualism and Support for Market Mechanisms," NBER working paper (2022).

Chapter Five

1. See, for instance, A. W. Cappelen, A. D. Hole, E. Ø. Sorensen and B. Tungodden, "The Pluralism of Fairness Ideals: An Experimental Approach," *American Economic Review* 97, no. 3 (2007): 818–27.
2. "Expert Report of Peter Arcidiacono," *Students for Fair Admissions v. Harvard* (2018).
3. This sentence is from the majority opinion written by Sandra Day O'Connor in the 2003 case, *Grutter v. Bollinger*, a case involving the University of Michigan. See Tiana Headley, "Harvard Admissions Case Tests O'Connor's 2003 Call on Race Bias," Bloomberg Law, August 11, 2021, https://news.bloomberglaw.com/us-law-week/harvard-race-admissions-case-tests-oconnors-25-year-prediction.
4. Available at https://www.supremecourt.gov/oral_arguments/audio/2022/20-1199.
5. Pew Research Center, "As Courts Weigh Affirmative Action, Grades and Test Scores Seen as Top Factors in College Admissions" (2022).
6. Lyndon B. Johnson, Commencement Address at Howard University: "To Fulfill These Rights," online by Gerhard Peters and John T. Woolley, The American Presidency Project, https://www.presidency.ucsb.edu/documents/commencement-address-howard-university-fulfill-these-rights.
7. In a clever experimental design, Andre asks "spectators" to evaluate the merit of "workers" who complete tasks. He finds that spectators tend to reward workers the

same way, whether or not these workers are told in advance about their incentives (pay per task). As a result, effort and merit could be different concepts, but in the minds of Andre's spectators, they are not. See Peter Andre, "Shallow Meritocracy," SAFE working paper 405 (2021).

8. See, for instance, John Roemer and Alain Trannoy, "Equality of Opportunity," in *Handbook of Income Distribution* (Elsevier, 2015), 217–300. Our discussion is based on the presentation in Alexander Cappelen, Erik Sørensen, and Bertil Tungodden, "Responsibility for What? Fairness and Individual Autonomy," *European Economic Review* (2010).
9. Cappelen, Sørensen, and Tungodden, "Responsibility for What?"
10. J. E. Roemer, "Equality of Opportunity: A Progress Report," *Social Choice and Welfare* (2002): 455–71.
11. R. Dworkin, *Sovereign Virtue: The Theory and Practice of Equality* (Harvard University Press, 2000).
12. Emily Oster, *The Family Firm* (New York: Penguin Books, 2022).
13. Kwame Anthony Appiah, "The Lies That Bind: Rethinking Identity," Eagleton Institute of Politics, Rutgers University, New Brunswick, NJ, March 29, 2019, presented by the Louis J. Gambaccini Civic Engagement Series and the Eagleton Institute of Politics at Rutgers University, https://www.youtube.com/watch?v=NOEHm2jM-sk.
14. Michael Sandel, *The Tyranny of Merit: What's Become of the Common Good?* (Macmillan, 2020). Long before Sandel and before the invention of the term "meritocracy," the French philosopher Simone Weil had anticipated this tension: "A certain combination of equality and inequality is constituted by the equality of possibilities. If anyone can reach the social rank corresponding to the function they are capable of fulfilling, and if education is widespread enough so that no one is deprived of any capacity by the mere fact of their birth, hope is the same for all children. . . . First, for a man who is in an inferior situation and who suffers from it, to know that his situation is caused by his incapacity, and to know that everyone knows it, is not a consolation, but a double offense; depending on character, some may be overwhelmed by it, others led to crime." See Weil, *Uprootedness: Prelude to a Declaration of the Duties of the Human Being* (Gallimard, 1949).
15. Shannon McKoy and Brenda Major, "Priming Meritocracy and the Psychological Justification of Inequality," *Journal of Experimental Social Psychology* 43, no. 3 (2007).
16. Stefanie Stantcheva, "Understanding Economic Policies: What Do People Know and Learn?," Harvard University working paper (2020).
17. Stefanie Stantcheva, "2020 Taxes and Policy Survey" (2021), unpublished paper, available at https://www.stefanie-stantcheva.com/research/Taxes_and_Policy_Survey_France.pdf.
18. Paola Sapienza and Luigi Zingales, "Economic Experts versus Average Americans," *American Economic Review* 103, no. 3 (2013): 636–42.
19. Sara Maestre-Andres, Stefan Drews, Savin Ivan, and Jeroen Van Der Bergh, "Carbon Tax Acceptability with Information Provision and Mixed Revenue Uses," *Nature Communications* (2021).
20. See Thomas Douenne and Adrien Fabre, "Yellow Vests, Pessimistic Beliefs and Carbon Tax Aversion," *American Economic Journal: Economic Policy* 14, no. 1 (2022): 81–110. In this paper, the authors inform survey participants about such a redistributive scheme, and ask if that changes their support for a carbon tax. They find effects to be small.
21. Megha Srivastava, Hoda Heidari, and Andrea Krause, "Mathematical Notions vs. Human Perception of Fairness: A Descriptive Approach to Fairness for Machine Learning," in *KDD '19: Proceedings of the 25th ACM SIGKDD International Conference on Knowledge Discovery & Data Mining* (ACM, 2019), 2459–68.

22. Danielle Li, Lindsey Raymond, and Peter Bergman, *Hiring as Exploration*, NBER Working paper 27736.
23. Srivastava, Heidari, and Krause, "Mathematical Notions vs. Human Perception of Fairness."

Chapter Six

1. Paola Sapienza and Luigi Zingales, "Economic Experts versus Average Americans," *American Economic Review* 103, no. 3 (2013): 636–42.
2. Christopher Johnson and Andrew Ballard, "Economists and Public Opinion: Expert Consensus and Economic Policy Judgments," *Journal of Politics* (2016).
3. Paul A. Samuelson, "The Way of an Economist," in *The Collected Scientific Papers of Paul A. Samuelson*, ed. Robert C. Merton, vol. 3 (MIT Press), 683.
4. Paul Krugman, *Peddling Prosperity: Economic Sense and Nonsense in the Age of Diminished Expectations* (W. W. Norton, 1995).
5. Dani Rodrik, "How to Save Globalization from Its Cheerleaders" (Harvard University working paper, 2007).
6. David H. Dorn, David Autor, and Gordon H. Hanson, "The China Syndrome: Local Labor Market Effects of Import Competition in the US," *American Economic Review* 103, no. 6 (2013).
7. Paul Krugman, "Globalization: What Did We Miss?," in *Meeting Globalization's Challenges*, ed. Luis Catão and Maurice Obstfeld (Princeton University Press, 2019).
8. EVS, *European Values Study 2017: Integrated Dataset (EVS 2017)*, (Cologne: GESIS, 2022), ZA7500 Data file version 5.0.0, https://doi.org/10.4232/1.13897.
9. Andrew Clark and Andrew Oswald, "A Simple Statistical Method for Measuring How Life Events Affect Happiness," *International Journal of Epidemiology* (2002).
10. Reshmaan Hussam, Erin M. Kelley, Gregory Lane, and Fatima Zahra, "The Psychosocial View of Employment," NBER working paper 28924 (2021).
11. Sapienza and Zingales, "Economists vs. Average Americans."
12. Rafael Di Tella and Dani Rodrik, "Labor Market Shocks and the Demand for Trade Protection: Evidence from Online Surveys," *Economic Journal* 130, no. 628 (2020): 1008–30.
13. Sahil Chinoy, Nathan Nunn, Sandra Sequeira and Stephanie Stantcheva, "Zero-Sum Thinking and the Roots of U.S. Political Divides," NBER working paper 31688 (2023).
14. Jonathan Haidt, "The Righteous Mind: Why Good People Are Divided by Politics and Religion" (Knopf, 2012). Haidt argues that, according to Durkheim, all four moral values (loyalty, authority, compassion, and fairness) are equally important to flourishing individuals. As we saw in chapter 4, the nineteenth-century French sociologist laments the loss of these values in modern society.
15. Readers interested in knowing more can go through the reference list in Oliver Hart, David Thesmar, and Luigi Zingales, "Private Sanctions," *Economic Policy* (2024).
16. Emmanuel Macron, "Discours à l'occasion du 78e anniversaire de la libération de Bormes-les-Mimosas," Bormes-les-Mimosas, Var, August 19, 2022.
17. Source: Briq Institute, "Germans' Willingness to Pay for Gas and Heating" (March 2022), https://www.briq-institute.org/media/briq_policy_monitor_01_en.pdf.
18. William MacAskill, *Doing Good Better: How Effective Altruism Can Help You Help Others, Do Work that Matters, and Make Smarter Choices about Giving Back* (Penguin, 2015).
19. David Atkin, Eve Colson-Sihra and Moses Shayo, "How Do We Choose Our Identity? A Revealed Preference Approach Using Food Consumption," *Journal of Political Economy* (2021).

20. See, for instance, Anne Effland, Mary Anne Normille, and John Wainio, "Global Agriculture and the Doha Round—Market Access Is the Key," Amber Waves, US Department of Agriculture, Economic Research Service, September 1, 2006.
21. Daniel Cohen and Thierry Verdier, "La mondialisation immatérielle," report of the Conseil d'Analyse Économique, La Documentation française, 2008.
22. The "Toubon law" from 1996.
23. David Card, "The Impact of the Mariel Boatlift on the Miami Labor Market," *Industrial and Labor Relations Review* 43, no. 2 (January 1990): 245–57.
24. See, for example, the very balanced presentation by Abhijit Banerjee and Esther Duflo, *Good Economics for Hard Times* (Public Affairs, 2019).
25. See, for instance, Ran Abramitzy, Philipp Ager, Leah Boustan, Elior Cohen and Casper Worm-Hansen, "The Effects of Immigration on the Economy: Lessons from the 1920s Border Closure," *American Economic Journal: Applied Economics* (2023).
26. See, for instance, Shai Bernstein, Rebecca Diamand, Abhisit Jiranaphawiboon, Timothy McQuade, and Beatriz Pousada, "The Contribution of High-Skilled Immigrants to Innovation in the United States," NBER working paper 30797 (2022).
27. Jens Hainmueller and Daniel Hopkins, "Public Attitudes towards Immigration," *Annual Review of Political Science* (2014).
28. Stefanie Stantcheva, "The Fog of Immigration" (Project Syndicate, 2018).
29. Hainmueller and Hopkins, "Public Attitudes towards Immigration."
30. *European Values Study 2017*.
31. The question is formulated as follows:

> A large number of jobs in agriculture, retail, hotels, and restaurants, are held by immigrants. Are you in favor of allowing immigrants to come to take these jobs? Please give a score of 1 (do not agree) to 10 (fully agree).
>
> List the main reasons for your response. Please select your answers in order of preference:
>
> 1. Immigrants are too different from me
> 2. Cultural diversity is a source of wealth
> 3. Immigrants create safety issues
> 4. Through their work, immigrants create wealth
> 5. Immigrants take our jobs
> 6. Immigrants cost our social services a lot
> 7. It is our duty to welcome foreigners who are struggling in their country
> 8. Immigrants take the jobs that employers have trouble filling
> 9. Other (specify)

32. Hainmueller and Hopkins, "Public Attitudes towards Immigration."
33. *European Values Study 2017*, questions 188 (On a scale of 1 to 4, how important is it that immigrants do not maintain distinct customs and traditions?); 192 (On a scale of 1 to 4, how important is it that immigrants speak the national language?); and 193 (On a scale of 1 to 4, how important is it that immigrants share the national culture?).
34. For a clear exposition of this view, see Ronald Inglehart, and Pippa Norris, "Trump, Brexit, and the Rise of Populism: Economic Have-Nots and Cultural Backlash," HKS Faculty Research Working Paper Series RWP16-026, August 2016.
35. Or at least one can say they are difficult to measure. In a famous 2012 paper, the economists Costas Arkolakis, Arnaud Costinot, and Andrés Rodríguez-Clare have estimated the gains from specialization at about 1 percent of GDP in the United States (compared with about 4 percent for European countries using a similar methodology).

Their methodology is robust to the type of model used, but not out of the range of simulations run by the WTO or during the Brexit debate. Why is the number so small? First, most countries are relatively "closed": most of their consumption comes from local production. Second, imports are exchange rate sensitive in the data, indicating that countries can easily "do without" foreign products. See Arkolakis, Costinot, and Rodríguez-Clare, "New Trade Models, Same Old Gains?," *American Economic Review* 102, no. 1 (February 2012): 94–130.

Chapter Seven

1. Emerson actually met Muir at the end of his life, when they camped together at Yosemite.
2. John Muir, preface to *Our National Parks* (1901).
3. Wikipedia, s.v. "Price elasticity of demand," en.wikipedia.org/wiki/Price_elasticity_of_demand.
4. Yet another angle to the price of the sublime: people accept lower salaries to become national park rangers, artists, museum curators or, for that matter, mathematicians, which shows implicitly the value they see in these activities compared to their other options.
5. In fact, the pleasure we get from consuming art might be reinforced by others consuming it, as we can then talk about it, compare notes, and so on.
6. Peter Singer, *The Most Good You Can Do* (Yale University Press, 2015).
7. Hannah Ginsborg, "Kant's Aesthetics and Teleology," in *The Stanford Encyclopedia of Philosophy* (Fall 2022 edition), ed. Edward N. Zalta and Uri Nodelman, https://plato.stanford.edu/entries/kant-aesthetics/.
8. It also differs from ethical judgment, in that it does not aim at producing more good in the world.
9. Bourdieu believed that "cultural education" for the masses is just a power move. Instead of genuinely educating the working class, it is more about making them feel small, so as to make the elite's dominance feel like the natural order.
10. Pierre Bourdieu, Alain Darbel, and Dominique Schnapper, *The Love of Art: European Museums and Their Public* (Stanford University Press, 1990).
11. Joseph A. Schumpeter, *History of Economic Analysis* (Routledge, 2006; originally published 1954), 126.
12. Anna Carabelli and Mario Cedrini, "Great Expectations and Final Disillusionment: Keynes, 'My Early Beliefs' and the Ultimate Values of Capitalism," *Cambridge Journal of Economics* (2018).
13. P. V. Mini, "The Anti-Benthamism of JM Keynes: Implications for The General Theory," *American Journal of Economics and Sociology* 50, no. 4 (1991): 453–68.
14. J. S. Mill, *Utilitarianism* (1863).
15. Agnes Callard, *Aspiration: The Agency of Becoming* (Oxford University Press, 2017).
16. J. S. Mill, "Utilitarianism," in *Collected Works of John Stuart Mill*, ed. J. M. Robson, vol. 10 (University of Toronto Press, 1985), 212.
17. "Public Opinion on National Parks," Center for American Progress (2016).
18. Roper Center for Public Opinion Research, "See America First: Public Opinion and National Parks."
19. Ronald Dworkin, *A Matter of Principle* (Harvard University Press, 1985), chap. 11.
20. C. G. J. Jacobi, Letter to A. M. Legendre, July 2, 1830, in *C. G. J. Jacobi's Gesammelte Werke*, vol. 1 (Reimer, 1881), 454–61.

21. F. Bastiat, "What Is Seen and What Is Not Seen" (1850), in *Selected Essays on Political Economy*, trans. S. Cain (Foundation for Economic Education, 1995).
22. Mario Vargas Llosa, "L'Exception culturelle?," in *Les Enjeux de la liberté* (Gallimard, 1997).
23. For instance, our own country, France, whose GDP is approximately 20 percent that of the United States, has a cultural budget equivalent to the US federal budget of parks and museums.

Chapter Eight

1. The polling firm Gallup has consistently asked the same question from 1973 to 2022. Results are reported on this webpage: https://news.gallup.com/poll/5248/big-business.aspx. The trust in small business is much higher: the fraction of participants who place little or no trust in small business has remained at 6 percent since the question was first asked, in 1997.
2. For a list, see Chief Executive Leadership Institute, "Over 1,000 Companies Have Curtailed Operations in Russia—But Some Remain," Yale School of Management, updated July 29, 2024, https://som.yale.edu/story/2022/over-1000-companies-have-curtailed-operations-russia-some-remain.
3. Milton Friedman, "The Social Responsibility of Business Is to Increase Its Profits," *New York Times*, September 13, 1970.
4. Lucian A. Bebchuk and Roberto Tallarita, "The Illusory Promise of Stakeholder Governance," Harvard Law School Forum on Corporate Governance, March 2, 2020, https://corpgov.law.harvard.edu/2020/03/02/the-illusory-promise-of-stakeholder-governance/.
5. Milton Friedman, "The Social Responsibility of Business Is to Increase Its Profits," *New York Times Magazine*, September 13, 1970.
6. Alex Edmans, *Grow the Pie: How Great Companies Deliver Both Purpose and Profits* (Cambridge University Press, 2020).
7. Rebecca Henderson, *Reimagining Capitalism in a World on Fire* (PublicAffairs, 2020).
8. Michael Hiscox, Jens Hainmueller, and Sandra Sequeira, "Consumer Demand for the Fair Trade Label: Evidence from a Multi-Store Field Experiment," *Review of Economics and Statistics* (2015).
9. See, for instance, the papers referenced in Lea Cassar and Stephan Meier, "Intentions for Doing Good Matter for Doing Well: The Negative Effects of Prosocial Incentives," *Economic Journal* 131, no. 637 (2021): 1988–2017.
10. Philipp Krüger, Daniel Metzger, and Jiaxin Wu, "The Sustainability Wage Gap," SSRN Working Paper (2022).
11. Raymond Fisman, Daniel Elfenbein, and Brian McManus, "Charity as a Substitute for Reputation: Evidence from an Online Marketplace," *Review of Economic Studies* (2012).
12. Lea Cassar and Stephan Meier, "Intentions for Doing Good Matter for Doing Well: The Negative Effects of Prosocial Incentives."
13. M. Amengual and E. P. Apfelbaum, "True Motives: Prosocial and Instrumental Justifications for Behavioral Change in Organizations," *Management Science* 67, no. 8 (2021): 5032–51.
14. R. F. Jensen, J. Aloysius, and C. Hofer, "When Words and Actions Don't Match: How Greenwashing a Firm's Supply Chain Practices Can Backfire," in *Academy of Management Proceedings* 2022, no. 1: 17262.
15. Russell Hotten, "Volkswagen: The Scandal Explained," BBC News, December 10, 2015, www.bbc.com/news/business-34324772.

16. See Bureau of Labor Statistics, "Nonprofits Account for 12.3 Million Jobs, 10.2 Percent of Private Sector Employment, in 2016" (2018).
17. Massachusetts Institute of Technology, "1.1 Mission and Objectives," MIT Policies, last updated October 18, 2022, https://policies.mit.edu/policies-procedures/10-institute/11-mission-and-objectives.
18. Michael Ewens, Arpit Gupta, and Sabrina T. Howell, "Local Journalism under Private Equity Ownership," NBER working paper (2022); Atul Gupta, Sabrina T. Howell, Constantine Yannelis, and Abhinav Gupta, "Does Private Equity Investment in Healthcare Benefit Patients? Evidence from Nursing Homes," *Review of Financial Studies* 37, no 4 (2024): 1029–77; Charlie Eaton, Sabrina Howell and Constantine Yannelis, "When Investor Incentives and Consumer Interests Diverge: Private Equity in Higher Education," *Review of Financial Studies* 33, no 9 (2020): 4024–60.
19. Jonathan Haidt, "Teen Mental Health Is Plummeting, and Social Media Is a Major Contributing Cause," Testimony to Senate Judiciary Committee (2022).
20. Roy Shapira and Luigi Zingales, "Is Pollution Value-Maximizing? The DuPont Case," NBER working paper 23866 (2017).
21. Business Roundtable, "Business Roundtable Redefines the Purpose of a Corporation to Promote 'An Economy That Serves All Americans'" (2019).
22. Lucian Bebchuk and Roberto Tallarita, "The Illusory Promise of Stakeholder Governance," SSRN working paper (2020).
23. E. Merrick Dodd Jr., "For Whom Are Corporate Managers Trustees?," *Harvard Law Review* (1932).
24. Luigi Zingales, "Don't Trust CEOs Who Say They Don't Care about Shareholder Value," *Washington Post*, August 20, 2019.
25. Ben & Jerry's, "Issues We Care About," https://www.benjerry.com/values/issues-we-care-about.
26. Wikipedia, "List of benefit corporations," last edited August 2, 2024, https://en.wikipedia.org/wiki/List_of_benefit_corporations.
27. Christopher Grimes, "Disney Chief's 'Don't Say Gay' Drama Is a Crisis of His Own Making," *Financial Times* (2022).
28. Patrick Temple-West, "Shareholders Bring the Abortion Battle into the Boardroom," *Financial Times* (2022).

Chapter Nine

1. A. O. Hirschman, *Exit, Voice, and Loyalty: Responses to Decline in Firms, Organizations, and States* (Harvard University Press, 1970).
2. J. Wesley, "The Use of Money," sermon 50, in *The Works of John Wesley*, ed. T. Jackson, 3rd ed., vol. 6 (1760; Wesleyan Methodist Book Room, 1872), 124–36.
3. W. H. Kaempfer, J. A. Lehman, and A. D. Lowenberg, "Divestment, Investment Sanctions, and Disinvestment: An Evaluation of Anti-apartheid Policy Instruments," *International Organization* 41, no. 3 (1987): 457–73.
4. S. P. Sethi and O. F. Williams, *Economic Imperatives and Ethical Values in Global Business: The South African Experience and International Codes Today* (University of Notre Dame Press, 2000), 143.
5. A. Falk, T. Neuber, and N. Szech, "Diffusion of Being Pivotal and Immoral Outcomes," *Review of Economic Studies* 87, no. 5 (2020): 2205–29.
6. See A. Liptak, "Supreme Court Rejects Purdue Pharma's Opioid Settlement," *New York Times*, March 21, 2024.

7. Jon Hale, "U.S. Sustainable Funds Continued to Break Records in 2020," *Morningstar*, February 25, 2021.
8. US SIF Foundation, *Report on US Sustainable and Impact Investing Trends 2022* (US SIF: The Forum for Sustainable and Responsible Investment, 2022).
9. R. Bauer, T. Ruof, and P. Smeets, "Get Real! Individuals Prefer More Sustainable Investments," *Review of Financial Studies* 34, no. 8 (2021): 3976–4043.
10. Joseph Keefe, "50 Years of Sustainable Investing at Pax World," *GreenMoney Journal* (September 2021), https://greenmoney.com/50-years-of-sustainable-investing-at-pax-world/.
11. Jonathan Berk and Jules H. Van Binsbergen, "The Impact of Impact Investing," SSRN working paper (2021).
12. A second reason why the price effect is small is more subtle. When traditional investors buy all stocks, they use brown stocks to diversify away some of the risks of green stocks. Green investors do not have this option and thus have a lower risk appetite. This attenuates their enthusiasm for green stocks. This attenuation effect is important because historically brown stocks offer useful diversification benefits. Note that this second effect, which rests on risk, is specific to financial markets. It does not operate on classic product markets.
13. This comes from the fact that, in their data, brown firms emit on average 1,300 tons per million dollars of revenue. For green firms, the same quantity is 5 tons. See Samuel M. Hartzmark and Kelly Shue, "Counterproductive Sustainable investing: The Impact Elasticity of Brown and Green Firms," SSRN working paper (2023).
14. J. F. Bonnefon, A. Landier, P. R. Sastry, and D. Thesmar, "The Moral Preferences of Investors: Experimental Evidence," NBER working paper 29647 (2022).
15. Andrew Browne, "ESG Whistleblower Calls Out Wall Street Greenwashing," Bloomberg, October 2, 2021, https://www.bloomberg.com/news/newsletters/2021-10-02/esg-whistleblower-calls-out-wall-street-greenwashing-new-economy-saturday.
16. See B. Biais and A. Landier, "Emission Caps and Investment in Green Technologies," SSRN working paper 4100087 (2022).

Afterword

1. Daniel M. Hausman, "Are Markets Morally Free Zones?," *Philosophy and Public Affairs* (1989): 317–33.

Index